BLACK WARRIORS:
THE BUFFALO SOLDIERS
OF WORLD WAR II

BLACK WARRIORS: THE BUFFALO SOLDIERS OF WORLD WAR II

MEMORIES OF THE ONLY NEGRO INFANTRY DIVISION TO FIGHT IN EUROPE DURING WORLD WAR II

BY

IVAN J. HOUSTON

WITH GORDON COHN

iUniverse, Inc.
Bloomington

Black Warriors: The Buffalo Soldiers of World War II
Memories of the Only Negro Infantry
Division to Fight in World War II

iUniverse books may be ordered through booksellers or by contacting:

iUniverse
1663 Liberty Drive
Bloomington, IN 47403
www.iuniverse.com
1-800-Authors (1-800-288-4677)

Because of the dynamic nature of the Internet, any Web addresses or links contained in this
book may have changed since publication and may no longer be valid.

ISBN: 978-1-9362-3640-4 (sc)
ISBN: 978-1-9362-3641-1 (ebook)

Library of Congress Control Number: 2011901498

Printed in the United States of America

iUniverse rev. date: 3/4/2011

It was my good fortune at Santiago to serve beside colored troops. A man who is good enough to shed his blood for the country is good enough to be given a square deal afterward. More than that no man is entitled to, and less than that no man shall have.

—Theodore Roosevelt

Once let the black man get upon his person the brass letter, U.S., let him get an eagle on his button, and a musket on his shoulder and bullets in his pocket, there is no power on earth that can deny that he has earned the right to citizenship.

—Frederick Douglass

CONTENTS

MAPS

American Negroes have fought and died in every war since the Revolution. They have also fought and died to achieve full citizenship. During the late 1930s, influential Negro individuals and organizations rose in response to the charge that the Black man was too dumb, lazy, or indifferent to serve in combat with his White brothers. Among the most influential and insistent in support of the Negro's quest for equality in what remained, by official White House policy, a segregated military were two major metropolitan newspapers, the *Chicago Defender* and *Pittsburgh Courier*. The *Defender*, founded in 1905 by Robert Sengstacke Abbott, became a strong voice in the fight against racism and segregation under the leadership of Abbott's nephew, John H. Sengstacke. The *Courier*, the largest of the nation's Negro newspapers, achieved national influence under Robert Lee Vann, editor-publisher, from 1910 to 1940, and had its greatest popularity under Ira Lewis. In 1938, the *Courier* published an open letter to President Franklin Delano Roosevelt and solicited public and government support for the establishment of an all-Negro division in the peacetime army. These two exemplars of the Negro press argued for equal treatment in those days and became strong voices in the fight against racism and segregation, urging, "Give our boys a chance to fight."

In 1942 Ira Lewis inaugurated the Double V program, which demanded that Blacks risking their lives overseas receive full citizenship at home.

AUTHOR'S NOTE

It was my great privilege and honor to serve in combat alongside the men of the 3rd Battalion, 370th Infantry Regimental Combat Team, 92nd Infantry Division of the U.S. Fifth Army between August 23, 1944, and May 2, 1945. The 92nd Division numbered fifteen thousand men during most of its time in combat. It fought alongside other U.S. troops, including Japanese-Americans and soldiers from Great Britain, Brazil, South Africa, and India. Ours was the only Negro division to fight as a unit in Europe during World War II. Our encounters with German forces in Italy over eight months began at the Arno River near little-known Cenaia and proceeded north through Pisa, Lucca, Seravezza, the Apennine mountains, Genoa, and the Po Valley.

In my position at battalion headquarters, I was partly responsible for the compilation of a minute-by-minute record of our unit's activities, which were assembled from continuous reports from men on the battlefield. Each battalion had a message center staffed by a runner from each company. Messengers carried information that could not be communicated by phone or radio.

The first entry in the journal of the 3rd Battalion, 370th Infantry Regiment, was delayed after our arrival and recorded beginning at 0030 hours (12:30 AM) on the morning of August 25, 1944. On that date the 3rd Battalion relieved a battalion of the 1st Armored Division near Pontedera, Italy, on the Arno River. The 3rd Battalion thus became the first American Negro infantry unit to engage in combat against Hitler's Nazi Germany in World War II.

Chiefly responsible for the journal and much that fills these pages was Sergeant Thomas T. Davis, a man of great organizational abilities, devotion, and honor. For the past sixty-plus years, I have kept in my home what I now believe to be the only copy of that journal outside the National Archives. In October 2007, I learned from the National Personnel Records Center of the National Archives and Records Administration that Sergeant Davis died on August 26, 2006. I regret that we never got together after the war to discuss our shared experience and what it meant in our later lives.

Now, in my eighty-fourth year, it seems an appropriate time to share the memories of a young California college student who enlisted in the United States Army in a time of national crisis and describe some of the historic encounters and achievements of his fellow Negro soldiers during a breakthrough period in American military history. These pages are dedicated to my fellow Buffalo Soldiers.

ACKNOWLEDGMENTS

This book has been pending for sixty-three years. It might never have been completed if I had not been introduced to Gordon Cohn by a mutual friend, attorney J. J. Brandlin. Mr. Cohn, who had already assisted thirty-two men and women in the completion of their life stories when we met in 2007, read what I had written and urged me to dig deeply into memory and call up the sights, sounds, smells, and feelings from the Italian battlefields more than six decades ago and incorporate them into my text. He edited every word I wrote and worked to make this text clearer and more precise. He brought into my work the observations of other participants and commentators familiar with the challenges and achievements of the 92nd Division. I will be forever grateful for his assistance, without which *Black Warriors* would not exist.

I also want to acknowledge the contribution of his wife Lois, who assembled and displayed the book's photos, gathered from a variety of sources. Lois independently imposed upon her cousins, Diane and Buddy Schwarzbach, who were visiting Florence from Chicago in the fall of 2007, asking them to travel to the American military cemetery there and capture on film the grave of one of my 3rd Battalion's heroic fallen officers.

Paul Cholodenko organized and reproduced the maps that illustrate the Italian mountains, villages, and valleys where my battalion fought.

Dr. Carolyn Ross Johnston, holder of the Elie Wiesel Endowed Professorship in Humane Letters at Eckerd College in St. Petersburg, Florida, twice read the manuscript line by line and provided invaluable editorial assistance in helping me make the book come alive. Few persons benefit so greatly from someone they have never met. Thank you, Carolyn.

Donald Naftulin, Donald Seigel, and Joseph Hartnett also provided generous editorial comment. I deeply appreciate their interest and help.

My family has been behind me in this project from the beginning. My wife of sixty-three years, Philippa Jones Houston, continually asked me, "When are you going to finish that book?" Our son Ivan Abbott, a designer and tester of the Army's Bradley Fighting Vehicle, provided invaluable computer assistance and photos when we visited the Italian battlefields together. Our daughters Pam and Kathi encouraged me to get on with the project.

Willard Z. Carr, an old acquaintance, read an early version of the manuscript and gave me his valuable observations. Lynn Merrit, retired president of the Life Office Management Association, continually encouraged me. Fellow UC Berkeley students from more than sixty years ago, Ralph Phillips and Kent Fisher, provided me with information on the status of Negroes following World War II. Harry Cox, who as a lieutenant commanded the mortar platoon of our battalion, helped me get things right. J. Curtis Foster, an old Buffalo Soldier, offered his encouragement; while Lyle Marshall, another Buffalo Soldier, read an early draft and encouraged me to finish "a story that must be told."

My long time friends, Steve Johns, Stanley Robertson, Lola and Herman Hendricks added advice and encouragement.

Joanne Morris, freelance writer, and Rutha Beamon of the National Archives, Still Picture Reference Team, both provided wonderful assistance.

Finally, I would like to acknowledge Patrick Sutton of The Printing Spot in Los Angeles for putting the final versions of text, photos, and maps together.

I. J. H.
Los Angeles
March 2009

PROLOGUE

No surviving member of Combat Team 370 of the 92nd Buffalo Division will ever forget August 23–24, 1944, the night we prepared to enter combat for the first time. Assembled on the south bank of the Arno River near Pontedera, Italy, not far from Pisa and the Ligurian Sea, we were a single untested Negro infantry regiment in a racially segregated U.S. Army, poised to fight against the retreating battle-wise forces of Germany's 16th Panzergrenadier Reichsfuehrer Division under the overall command of Field Marshal Albert Kesselring. Once Hermann Göring's deputy, "Smiling Albert" had commanded Germany's air fleets during the invasion of France and the Battle of Britain in 1940 and later served as General Erwin Rommel's codirector of Germany's North African campaign. Acknowledged as one of the ablest strategists in the German high command, Kesselring was in Italy to direct a last-ditch defensive effort for a dying army. The Germans had lost Rome to the Allies just sixty days before and had retreated north to a deeply fortified position known as the Gothic Line; this position stretched 170 miles from the Ligurian Sea east across the Apennine mountains that form the spine of Italy to the Adriatic.

Who were we? A regimental combat team of four thousand men, predominantly Southern Negroes of modest education. We were select officers and men charged with preparing the way for the remainder of the 92nd Division, which would follow in our footsteps. All of our senior officers were White, and they were mostly Southern. Our junior officers were Negroes, mostly college men. We had arrived in Naples, Italy, only three weeks before and now were faced with a front that stretched along the Arno. Beside us were the famed 1st Armored Division, the Sixth South African Division, and support units that included the 68th and 91st Field Artillery Battalions and the 1st and 4th Tank Battalions.

Our assignment was to cross the Arno and break through the Gothic Line. We had been told that the Germans would infiltrate our positions and that some of them would speak American English in an effort to gain information from our soldiers. We were also told that British Indian troops would sneak up behind us and cut our throats if they did not notice the dogtag chain around our necks. We were green and nervous, yet somehow I felt no fear. I was beginning a great adventure. I believed that all the soldiers around me were capable and that we could handle the Germans. I wanted very much to be a significant part of a successful combat operation. It never crossed my mind that I might be killed or badly wounded. I was nineteen years old.

PREPARATION

On Sunday morning, December 7, 1941, I went downtown with my brother Norman and stepbrother, Hayward Thompson, to catch an early movie at the RKO Hill Street Theater at 8th and Hill Streets in Los Angeles. The name of the movie is long forgotten but I recall clearly that its projection was suddenly stopped and a civilian—perhaps the theater manager—came out onto the stage and announced that all servicemen should return to their bases immediately. The Japanese had bombed Pearl Harbor. I was sixteen years old, a senior at Polytechnic High School in Los Angeles, and I had no idea where Pearl Harbor was. I really didn't understand that this was the beginning of a major war.

Six months later, in June of 1942, I graduated from Poly. Because my father had attended the University of California at Berkeley, it was my intention to do so as well. (Norman had entered Cal the year before.) In those simpler days, a B+ average in an academic major and a class standing among the top 12.5 percent among California high school graduates were sufficient to get you into Cal. I managed that, majoring in math and science and earning varsity letters in both football and track, where I was a high jumper and hurdler.

When I arrived on the Berkeley campus, I moved into Oxford Hall, one of the student cooperative housing units. Tuition then was a modest $27.50 per semester, and room and board was only

1

$47. To make ends meet, I worked at least four hours a week at the co-op, washing dishes, clearing tables, and becoming an assistant cook. Housing in the student cooperatives was fully integrated; six of Oxford Hall's approximately one hundred residents were Negroes.

I entered the university with the idea that I would become a business administration major. All undergrads were required to spend their first two years as students in the College of Letters, Arts and Sciences, and I planned to enter the business school in my junior year. As a freshman, my grades were mostly Bs and Cs, with a sprinkling of As. I earned a letter on the freshman track-and-field team, achieving the height of six feet three inches in the high jump. I took boxing as a physical education elective, and as a light-heavyweight I fought and won several fights leading up to the fight for the university championship. I lost to a senior in that bout, but along the way I learned a great deal about boxing, especially that you had to be in tip-top condition to fight even a few rounds.

I became a member of the Reserve Officers Training Corps (ROTC) and was promoted to corporal after my second semester. During our ROTC classes, our instructors would frequently show us newsreels of the British fighting the Germans in North Africa. We had read about the aerial combat over London in the Battle of Britain. We also read about the battles in the Pacific. The war was definitely on our minds. You couldn't escape it; it was all around you. My brother Norman was drafted near the end of 1942 and entered the army at the beginning of 1943. He had been among the first Negroes to earn a varsity football letter at Cal.

One day early in 1943, I read on a campus bulletin board that anyone who enlisted in the army before he was eighteen would get a six-month deferment. Since I was seventeen, I thought it would be better for me to enlist because I knew that if I was drafted I would probably be gone within a month. When the semester at Cal ended in late May, I returned home to Los Angeles, and while downtown late one night I was confronted by a group of White sailors looking for trouble. I had arrived during what would become known as the Zoot Suit Riots, where young Mexican Americans and White sailors confronted and assaulted each other. The sailors' attentions also turned to Negro Americans because we, too, wore zoot suits. I was a convenient target. Their threat was sufficient for me to jump onto the first available streetcar, not one I would usually have taken, in order to get out of there and home in one piece.

I became a member of the Enlisted Reserve Corps on June 14, 1943, and received my army serial number—19203794—at that time, before returning to complete another semester at Berkeley. The university went on a war schedule in the summer of '43, scheduling three semesters a year. I began my third semester in July 1943 but left the campus after that term because I was called to active duty on January 3, 1944.

My mother and father had divorced in 1936. I returned to the home I had shared with my mother, grandmother, and Norman at 950 E. 42nd Place, about two long blocks east of Wrigley Field, home of the Los Angeles Angels, then a Chicago Cubs–owned minor league baseball team, and one short block from Central Avenue, the heart of the Negro community in Los Angeles. My father, Nornan O. Houston, had his office at Golden State Mutual Life Insurance Company, just one block away.

On January 3, 1944, my mother drove me the twenty-five miles down to San Pedro and dropped me off near Fort MacArthur, which had been an army training center since World War I. We had been told to bring little more than our toothbrush. As I walked down the path leading to the front gate of the induction center, I heard someone from a far-off barrack yell, "Hey, Jody, they got your ass now!" I was to learn later that every civilian

3

coming into the military was called Jody. It was the name used frequently during the calls-and-responses of marching drills.

It was at Fort MacArthur that I experienced the first segregation of my life. All the Negroes went into one company; everyone else into another. I was not really surprised because I had heard of the situation from my brother and others. We knew that the U.S. Army was segregated everywhere around the world. Men who had not yet received one were given their serial numbers. We were given uniforms, and the Negro soldiers were assigned to segregated barracks of about one hundred men, almost all from Southern California. I was in Company B. There was no interaction with the other barracks; we remained strictly segregated and ate with other Negro recruits. Some of the men were as young as I, but others seemed to have been in the army for a while and were in their mid-thirties. Some were being treated for syphilis or other venereal diseases, and they warned us about the shots we were about to be given. I was told that one of the shots for syphilis was administered with a very long needle. We did receive shots soon afterward, but they were for typhoid and tetanus, administered with ordinary needles. Nevertheless, our arms were sore for days afterward.

The terms "nigger" and "motherfucker" were quite common in our barracks. Some of my friends in the neighborhood used those terms, but they were never spoken anywhere near my home. In my family we never even used the word "damn." My friends in the neighborhood did, however, play a vicious word game called "The Dozens," which centered on each other's mothers. For example, one guy might say, "Your mother is so bowlegged she doesn't have to spread her legs to get on a horse." The other fellow might respond, "Your mother *is* the horse." Most of us would stand around and laugh, and nobody got into a fight over the game. Talk in the barracks was much like that. There was a lot of horseplay, and many of the words that were used were coded so that "Mr. Charlie," the White man and the real boss in the army, would not understand.

I was the only college student in the Negro barracks. I talked differently from the rest, and this caused some of the inductees to view me in a strange light. They began to pick on me. One guy challenged me to a fight only two or three days after our arrival at Fort MacArthur. I was a college boy, and he was a street kid. I was six feet one inch tall, 185 pounds, and had always been a good athlete. Joe Louis, the "Brown Bomber" and heavyweight champion of the world, was one of my idols. I used the boxing experience I had gained at Cal and beat the stew out of my opponent until he quit. Afterward, we became friends. The others left me alone after that.

During my stay at Fort MacArthur, we saw a number of army training films. It seemed that every other film was on venereal disease. A soldier would get court-martialed if he contracted VD, and those films were meant to scare the hell out of us. We saw endless pictures of men with the pox, with syphilis and gonorrhea, and learned what happened to the body during each stage of those diseases. I was also introduced to my first "short-arm" examination at Fort MacArthur. The sergeant and an officer would awaken us in the middle of the night. Each soldier's private parts were examined by flashlight, and he was told to "milk down" his member. Notes were made of the findings on each soldier, and those caught with suspected sores or drippings were called out of line. An awful lot of kidding went on during those examinations.

Soon everyone took the Army General Classification Test (AGCT) and a test of mechanical aptitude. When the test results were announced, I learned that my scores were good in both—and according to the administrator, "out of sight" on the mechanical aptitude test. They told me that I was being assigned to the Army Specialized Training Corps (ASTP). I had hoped to become a pilot in the U.S. Army Air Force. I knew some of the members of the 99th Pursuit Squadron, all Negro, who later became famous as the Tuskegee Airmen after their achievements against enemy aircraft over North Africa, Italy, and Sicily. One member of the 99th—Louis Curtis Smith—grew up on the same block as I did. He got shot down twice and became a prisoner of war the second time.

Instead of being sent to join an air force program, I was told that I was being sent to Fort Benning, Georgia, for infantry basic training as part of the ASTP. They said that after those chosen for the ASTP completed basic training, they would be sent to one of the nation's colleges—in my case, a Negro college—to earn an engineering degree before being commissioned a second lieutenant.

Thirty of us who had been chosen for the ASTP boarded a sleeping-car train at Fort MacArthur. Emmett Chapell, a college boy from Phoenix, Arizona, and I were the only Negroes. A White lieutenant was assigned to take us from Fort MacArthur to Fort Benning. At that point we had been given no military training. We had done only kitchen police work and learned how to make our beds according to army standards. The blanket on a bed made according to army standards will cause a coin to bounce six inches high. If the coin does not bounce that high, the barrack sergeant will pull the bed apart and demand that it be made over. All recruits were assigned to clean the grounds of the army base. We were not released to our barracks if there was even so much as a matchstick found in our assigned cleaning area.

Our train from Fort MacArthur moved slowly through Los Angeles and stopped at Union Station on Alameda Street. I had been able to notify my parents when we would be arriving, and they both came to visit. Too quickly we said our good-byes, and later my mother told me that was the first time she had seen my father cry. Our sleeping car joined the regular passenger train—

The Sunset Limited—headed for New Orleans. We pulled out on January 17, 1944. Chapell and I bunked together. We slept with our heads at opposite ends of the bunk. Ours was the only military car, and all thirty recruits joined the civilian passengers in the dining car for meals.

Before we had left Los Angeles, my mother (a native Angeleno) told me, "Don't even look out the train window when you are in Mississippi. Those White people just don't like Negroes." But it was in El Paso, well before we reached the Deep South, that Jim Crow first appeared. We saw the segregation of the races during our brief stop there. From that point on, Chapell and I continued to eat in the dining car, but a curtain was placed around our table. We reached New Orleans around noon and learned that we would not be continuing to Fort Benning until that evening. The White lieutenant who took our military detail on this train trip apparently did not know how Southerners felt about Negroes or did not think that Southern state laws affected soldiers. He took us to a restaurant near the train station. I was near the rear of the line, and word was soon passed back to me that Chapell, who was up ahead, would not be served. He was darker-skinned than I was. Chapell went down the street and found a place to eat on his own. I continued in line wondering what would happen, and I *was* served. I ate quickly and left. Chapell and I spent our few free hours in the Crescent City touring Xavier University with a student, Lorraine Fredericks, who later married my brother Norman.

Our next stop was Birmingham, Alabama. Again we thirty recruits left the train for lunch. The lieutenant took us to the Hotel Bankhead and a private dining room where all the Negro waiters kept staring at us as we ate with our White fellow recruits. Several sets of eyes were on Chapell and me. After an uneventful lunch, we walked back to the train station, noticing carloads of rough-looking white boys suddenly cruising the streets around us. Many years later I learned that the notorious Theophilus

Eugene "Bull" Connor, who served two terms as Birmingham's police commissioner between 1936 and 1952, had learned about our eating at the hotel and had called some of his boys to get us. A Birmingham woman I met later told me that the incident made the Birmingham papers. Fortunately, nothing serious developed, and we were soon back on the train and on our way to Ft. Benning, a huge military complex on the red soil of eastern Georgia.

We arrived on January 23, 1944, and were immediately assigned to barracks. As we were standing in line to get our bedding, it was obvious they were looking for the two Negroes among the rest of the recruits. Chapell had received his allocation, and they were looking for the other Negro. A dark Italian guy was in line ahead of me. They asked him, "Are you the other colored guy?" When he made it clear he was not, I identified myself.

Chapell and I entered a barracks and met four other Negro soldiers: Barry Seixas of Berkeley, California; Charlie Mack from Cleveland; James Good of Detroit; and another fellow I remember only as Jitterbug, who hailed from New York. The next day our barracks was filled with White recruits. We were all part of an ASTP company of nearly two hundred recruits. All of us were eighteen years old, and all had scored highly on the AGCT.

The company was formed into four platoons of forty-eight men, and each platoon consisted of four squads of a dozen men. We six Negroes were half of one squad. Seixas was chosen our squad leader. When we went to mess hall, we saw that Negroes were assigned to a segregated table. We quickly complained to our platoon leader, a White Southern second lieutenant from The Citadel, the military college of South Carolina, and after a week we were told we could eat wherever we wished in the mess hall. The lieutenant actually had called each of us Negro soldiers into his office and asked how we had been treated. In addition to remarking about the segregated seating arrangement, I told him that the mess sergeant, who had said he was from California, told each Negro soldier on KP duty that he would be responsible for keeping the kitchen coal fires burning. The lieutenant said that would not happen again.

Fort Benning was to be our home for thirteen weeks. All of the ASTP recruits continued to believe that we were eventually headed off to college for engineering study and commissions because Secretary of War Henry Stimson believed that the army needed engineering officers. In the meantime, we did a lot of marching, some of it double-time. As we marched we sang. The songs were typically stupid:

My bonnie lies over the ocean

My bonnie lies over the sea

My bonnie lies over the ocean

Your son's in the ASTP, T.S.

A-S-T-P, your son's in the ASTP, T.S.

A-S-T-P, your son's in the ASTP, T.S.

T.S., of course, stood for "tough shit."

We took many tests, studied maps, and learned the fundamentals of hand-to-hand combat and how to use gas masks. We had to sit in a building full of gas with our masks on. We learned that soldiers should never cross a bridge in step. The force of being in step could cause a bridge to collapse. We were to cross in what was called "route step," which really meant "out of step." We were told how certain poison gases smelled. I still remember that lewisite, a chemical agent that contains arsenic and is known to cause blistering of the skin, smelled like newly mowed hay. We learned how to use the bayonet and how to take apart, clean, and put our weapons together while blindfolded. We had night-training exercises and learned how to find our way in darkness.

We Negroes had no problems with any of the officers or other enlisted men. Toilets and drinking fountains were not segregated. However, we had to shop at a separate post exchange (PX), and when we went to the movies on the base we had to sit in the Negro section. A good friend of mine, Artie Ricmond, of Oakland, California, was in another ASTP company at Ft. Benning. Artie was passing for White. Artie sat with me in the Negro section. (Later he became a physician in Northern California.)

On a two-day pass, I took a bus to Tuskegee, Alabama, and visited with cousins. They took me to the campus of Tuskegee Institute and pointed out the laboratory of Dr. George Washington Carver (1864–1943), the famous Negro agriculture specialist and humanist.

Our scheduled thirteen weeks of basic training ended abruptly after only eight weeks. In March of 1944 the army suddenly announced the shutdown of the ASTP. Our forces overseas were experiencing heavy casualties in North Africa, Italy, and the Pacific, and preparations were underway for an invasion of Europe, which would certainly mean even more casualties. Manpower was needed *now*. All of us in the ASTP received word that we were being assigned to infantry divisions. We six Negroes were being sent to the 92nd Infantry Division, which was on maneuvers in Louisiana. The division had taken the name "Buffalo Soldiers" that the Indians had assigned to Black troops in the 1880s. The 92nd was the only Negro infantry division in the United States at the time. The only other Negro combat division, the 93rd, had been sent to the South Pacific in January 1944 and was fighting on Bougainville.

We went by train and then by army truck to the replacement depot of the 92nd Division in west-central Louisiana near Leesville and Merryville. There were no permanent structures at the camp, just a collection of tents far out in the woods. We saw no civilians and no sign of any town. I was given a physical, and the Negro army physician said my blood pressure was high; he thought I should transfer from a combat unit to a service unit, which meant a desk job somewhere. I must have been nuts, but I insisted on remaining in the combat unit. The doctor told me I was the only person he had ever talked to who demanded to be assigned to a combat unit. At the time I had no idea how much walking I would do as an infantryman. When I found out, I tried, without success, to transfer to the artillery.

Several soldiers, including me, were sent to Headquarters Company, 3rd Battalion, 370th Infantry Regiment. Headquarters was in a heavily wooded area. A White first lieutenant, Hugh D. Shires, commanding officer of Headquarters Company, 3rd Battalion, greeted us and shouted, "Does any one of you recruits know how to read maps?" I said I did and mentioned that I had finished three semesters of ROTC at Berkeley. Shires told me I would be an S-2 scout observer (S-2 was Intelligence) and would assist Staff Sergeant Thomas T. Davis, who was the operations sergeant. Shires took me to meet Davis, a Pennsylvanian, who showed me to the four-man shelter tent I would share with him and First Sergeant Edward S. Ross. I would remain a member of the 3rd Battalion Headquarters Company for the next twenty-one months, the balance of my army career. All men in the division below the rank of second lieutenant were Negroes.

I slept only one night at the bivouac location. Early the next morning the battalion moved out on foot toward a simulated enemy location. We were to engage in combat maneuvers against another division. I was carrying my rifle and full field pack. We walked all day and half the night, much of it through a cold rain. The wind was blowing, and the temperature dropped. We were freezing. We were not permitted to light fires for fear of revealing our location to the "enemy." That was the worst night I have ever experienced. I have never been colder than I was in western Louisiana.

At daybreak the next morning we learned that maneuvers had already ended. We camped near Merryville. While we were there, a large number of Negro ASTP soldiers from universities like Fisk and Howard joined the 92nd Division. Their education, like mine, had stopped with cancellation of the ASTP. We all had something in common: we had been to college. The rumor started that we had been sent to the 92nd to elevate its intelligence level to the point that would qualify the division for combat duty. I did not believe that was true, even though a large number of enlisted men in the division were semiliterate and some of them illiterate. They had to be taught to read and then made to understand maps and field manuals. I was unaware until I read many years later in Hondon B. Hargrove's *Buffalo Soldiers in Italy: Black Americans in World War II* that "a large number of men were inept, poorly motivated, or physically and/or emotionally unsuited for service" and were designated for so-called Casual Camps at Fort Huachuca, Arizona. These camps focused on special training intended to make the men combat ready. Hargrove says there were two thousand such men in the division in August 1944. Hundreds, Hargrove says, were "dumped" (p. 7) into the 92nd Infantry Division. (Hargrove served as a captain in the 597th Field Artillery of the 92nd Division during the Italian campaign.) He reports that 850 men deemed unsuitable for combat were sent overseas in the 92nd Division by War Department orders despite Major General Edward M. Almond's protest. I was not familiar with the term "Casual Camps." I did know, however, that there were guys who were trying to get out of duty. They did not want to stay in the army; they did not want to go overseas. I knew one guy who walked with a bent back all the time I was at

Ft. Huachuca. I don't know whether he was acting or not, but his back was bent almost at a 90-degree angle.

The 92nd Division, comprising nearly fifteen thousand men, consisted of three regiments: our 370th, the 365th, and the 371st. Each regiment included three battalions of about nine hundred men each. The 370th Regiment was commanded by Colonel Raymond G. Sherman, who had previously led the military band at the Presidio of San Francisco. In time our regiment was to become known as "Sherman's Raiders." Our 3rd Battalion numbered 854 men and was divided into five companies: I, K, L, M, and Headquarters Company. Commanding officer of the 3rd Battalion was Lieutenant Colonel Clarence W. Daugette Jr., a reserved and soft-spoken White man, formerly an insurance salesman and a leader of the Alabama National Guard. He was about five feet eleven inches tall and of medium build, and he had a strong Southern accent.

Of the five companies that constituted the 3rd Battalion, I Company, which was a rifle company, was commanded by a youthful and handsome Negro officer, Jesse Jarman. He was a first lieutenant when we went overseas, but after a month or two in combat he was promoted to captain. I never had much direct conversation with him, but he was obviously very intelligent, a natural leader; and like the other officers, he carried himself in a way that earned our respect. K Company was commanded by Captain Elmer F. Reedy, a White officer, possibly from the South. I didn't have much communication with him, either. Like the other company commanders, he would come to headquarters and talk to the colonel, but I was not part of that. L Company was headed by Lieutenant Clarence Brown, a Negro. He was slim and about six feet tall. Some of the officers called him "Pop-Off" Brown because he was a very outspoken guy. Like Jarman, he was a first lieutenant when we went overseas but became a captain soon afterward. When we went overseas, there were no Black company commanders who were captains. But within thirty to sixty days, Jarman and Brown were promoted by the regimental commander, R. G. Sherman. Colonel Daugette probably recommended them for promotion, and Sherman approved it. Company M was commanded by Lieutenant Julian Miles, a Negro officer, very straight and very efficient. His company was the 3rd Battalion's heavy weapons company. They had .50-caliber water-cooled machine guns and 81-mm mortars. Colonel Daugette particularly liked Captain Miles; and later, after our disastrous February 1945 attack in the Italian campaign, when they transferred out all the Black company commanders, I know that Colonel Daugette was very unhappy that Miles was gone. To a degree Miles had catered to the colonel.

Hargrove says in *Buffalo Soldiers in Italy* (p. 8) that from the beginning there was "an intangible, elusive undercurrent of resentment, bitterness, even despair and hopelessness among black officers and enlisted men in the 92nd. Most of it had to do with segregation and discrimination in messes, officers clubs and living quarters." In my battalion headquarters company and platoon, where I spent most of my time, I didn't hear or sense anything like that. I can imagine that the Negro officers who faced segregation every day, who had to go to a separate Negro club, would have been resentful, but since all of us enlisted men were Negroes we experienced no *sudden* sense of segregation. We were segregated from the moment we were assigned to the division.

Hargrove adds (p. 8), "Many men did not know their commanders' names." That was not the case in my battalion at the beginning of our days in combat, but when we began to experience casualties among our commanders and platoon leaders, and replacements began coming in, I am certain that the replacements would not have known their battalion commanders' names. They might have known that they were in a particular company of the 3rd Battalion, but nothing more. And they surely would not have known that Colonel Daugette was our commanding officer.

My transition from a student at the fully integrated University of California at Berkeley and Oxford Hall, where we danced with white girls from the other co-ops, to an infantry soldier in the fully segregated 92nd Division caused me no great frustration or anxiety. I knew in advance that this was the crazy way the army operated. I figured that once I was reassigned, I would do what I had to do—even though I was miserable doing it. I never wanted to be in the infantry because I did not like to walk. We were walking all over west-central Louisiana eight hours a day. It was raining constantly, and my feet were always wet. Serving with me in the S-2 Intelligence Squad of Headquarters Company were Fortunatus Sweeney from New Jersey; Zane Grey Phoenix of Steelton, Pennsylvania; Robert Turner from Kansas; and Jim Tucker from Texas. Each had a good education and was smart, and all had the good fortune to survive the war. Many of the other men with us in Leesville—most of the original fifteen thousand—were from the Deep South and, as I have written, were illiterate or barely able to read. Lieutenant Shires, our Headquarters Company commander, who had been a banker in Maryland before the war, was promoted to captain. He seemed to seek the smartest soldiers he could find, and our headquarters group reflected his selection.

The food in the field was terrible; on maneuvers and away from barracks a mobile mess kitchen was set up, and the mess sergeant, Atkerson, and his assistants, James W. P. Jones and Dupree, cooked and dished out food into our mess kits and canteen cups. Stew, powdered eggs, and creamed chipped beef laced with peas and carrots on toast (called SOS or "shit on a shingle") seemed ever present. Hot water was always there for washing the mess kits, which included a knife, fork, and spoon.

When maneuvers were over we boarded a troop train and headed slowly west to Ft. Huachuca in southeast Arizona. We took all meals while rolling along and were let off twice a day to exercise briefly, stretching and running around the train. Ft. Huachuca, home base of the 92nd Division, had been established in 1877, during the Apache Indian wars, when the army was chasing Geronimo (1829–1909). It was situated in isolation between Huachuca City and Sierra Vista, about seventy-five miles south of Tucson. During World War I, Ft. Huachuca had served the Buffalo Soldiers of the 10th Cavalry, comprised of Negro troops who guarded the United States–Mexico border. The fort site had been selected because of its high ground and abundance of trees and fresh water. We were following into Ft. Huachuca the Negro 93rd Division, now in the South Pacific.

When we arrived, on April 3, 1944, we were all astonished to see it snowing in the desert. Reveille was at 5:45 AM. First Sergeant Edward Ross, fully dressed, neatly pressed, always immaculate, would come through the barracks yelling, "Every living ass and every swinging dick, on your feet." We fell out in formation by platoons and made the morning report. Lieutenant Shires was the company commander, but in every company it is the first sergeant who actually runs the company.

Battalion Headquarters Company, which S-2 (Intelligence) was part of, was comprised of a headquarters platoon consisting of administration, operations, scouts, supplies, cooks, and clerks; a communications platoon made up of telephone and radio specialists; an antitank platoon, whose men operated four 37-mm antitank guns; and an ammunition and pioneer (A&P) platoon, whose members laid and exploded mines, used Bangalore torpedoes to blow barbed wire, dug latrines, and secured water. The S-1 (adjutant), S-2, S-3 (operations), and S-4 (supply) officers and functions were also part of Headquarters Platoon. Lieutenant L. C. Lucas commanded the communications platoon; Lieutenant

Harold Brooks, the A&P platoon; and Lieutenant Brown, the antitank platoon. All were Negroes.

The infantry lives on its feet, and the soldiers of the 3rd Battalion were great walkers. Wearing a full field pack we had to walk five miles in one hour, nine miles in two hours—which is fast and very hard—and twenty-five miles in eight hours. These training marches were done in the high Arizona desert with temperatures near one hundred degrees. Our full pack consisted of our weapon, half a shelter—it took two men to build a tent—a blanket, toilet articles, a canteen, and several clips of ammunition. We wore leggings then and did not get combat boots until we reached Italy. Our steel helmet had a liner; the helmet itself was used for washing up and shaving. They didn't want us to light fires on it because they said it would weaken the steel. There was also room in our pack for a Bible or other books of our choice. I carried a book on calculus written by Granville and Langley. At Cal I had received an F in calculus. I never understood its concepts and stubbornly refused to accept help. I was determined to make up for my embarrassment; and from time to time during my months in the army, I would study and read when there was nothing else to do. The army, however, liked to keep its soldiers very busy. Even in combat there were always assignments to clean and to train, and often we were dead tired from walking and climbing hills. I did a lot of reading when we were moving from place to place by ship, by truck, or by train. After the war, when I returned to Berkeley, I took the calculus course again and received an A.

At Ft. Huachuca I learned how to fire the standard ten-pound semi-automatic Garand M-1 rifle, the smaller and lighter .30-caliber carbine, and the .45-caliber pistol. I spent many hours assembling, disassembling, and cleaning those weapons and shooting from four principal positions: prone, sitting, kneeling, and standing. I was good with the M-1 and the carbine but not able to hit much with the .45.

As part of our training we were ordered to attack a mock combat village that had been built in the desert. Figures would jump up, and you either had to bayonet or shoot them. We waded across the San Pedro River; and because the air was so hot and dry, were able to sit fully submerged in the river, get up, and be completely dry in five minutes. I learned to love the desert, especially at sunrise and sunset. At sunrise the air was cool, still, and dry. Then reveille would break the silence, and the Buffalo Soldiers started their day. Sunsets were spectacular, and the sky filled with many colors. Sometimes the beauty was so great it could bring tears to my eyes.

In April, as we continued our training, we learned that we were to be part of Combat Team 370, which was created on April 4, 1944, by General Orders Number 14. Combat Team 370 included the 370th Infantry Regiment, the 598th Field Artillery Battalion, a company of engineers from the 317th Engineering Battalion, and a company of medics from the 317th Medical Battalion. The combat team would be commanded by Colonel Raymond G. Sherman and would be heading overseas in June 1944. We were to be the advance guard for the rest of the division.

I was sent to special school for two days at Ft. Huachuca to learn how to use a movie projector and became the official projectionist of the 3rd Battalion. I showed many army training and fighting films, including several on venereal diseases, along with commercial films for the pure entertainment of the troops. The most memorable was *The Negro Soldier*, much of which had been filmed at Ft. Huachuca using soldiers of the 92nd Division. The film ended on a high emotional note. We Negro soldiers knew we were ready to fight the armies of the Axis powers: Germany, Italy, and Japan. The army did a good job of teaching me about movie projectors. Many years later, returning on a TWA flight from a board meeting in New York City, I was seated in the first-class cabin when the projector broke down during an exciting film. Although it was out of sight, mounted in the ceiling of the aircraft, the projector turned out to be similar to those we had used in the army. I told the stewardess I could fix it. She said okay, and to the amazement of everyone in the cabin I had the film projected again in five minutes. One of my friends from the California Chamber of Commerce was aboard, and he had to tell all his friends what had happened at 37,000 feet.

In succeeding days we participated in firing maneuvers that were designed to prepare us to attack under our own artillery fire. We had to crawl under live machine-gun fire and throw grenades. When grenades explode, the sound is like a lot of bees swarming. Grenade fragments sometimes came down and hit us on our steel helmets. I felt no sense of fear during the war games. As a matter of fact, it was sort of fun. Bayonet training was something else. I hated it. We were ordered to hold up an M-1 rifle with bayonet attached and our arms stretched out in the crucifixion position; it was a test to see how long we could maintain the position. A ten-pound rifle gets to weigh a ton pretty quickly.

We marched in several parades before military dignitaries and on one occasion had the privilege to pass before General Almond, commanding general of the 92nd Infantry Division, and General of the Army George Catlett Marshall. We always looked sharp, the army band was consistently good, and the music always stirring. I believe I saw the 92nd's buffalo mascot one time when we were on parade.

There was regular chapel service at Ft. Huachuca, but I didn't attend. I don't know why. My brother and I had attended a Christian Science Sunday School until we entered college. I always believed that the universe was formed by a supreme being. From time to time Norman and I would attend other churches, and we had a great respect for other people's religious beliefs.

Little formal entertainment was available at Ft. Huachuca. Negro and White officers had separate officers' clubs and separate mess halls. The Negro Officers' Club was said to feature great jazz and other outstanding entertainment, but we enlisted men saw none of that when we were off duty; instead, we went to the movies or played cards at the PX or in the barracks. There was much gambling with dice and cards on every payday. I didn't hang around the gamblers. If men were lucky enough to get a brief pass, they might head to the neighboring community of Fry, where there were prostitutes, or over to Nogales and across the border to Agua Prieta in Sonora, Mexico, another place where women were available for a price.

I was at Ft. Huachuca on June 6, 1944, when we got word of the Normandy invasion. We followed the Allies' advance through the military newspaper, *Stars and Stripes*, but it didn't have any impact upon us. It meant only that we were not likely to be used in that field of operations.

During my time in Arizona, I received one ten-day pass and left for Los Angeles by train from Tucson. I visited with family and one day drove my mother's car, a gray 1937 Plymouth, to the campus of UCLA to see friends who had not been drafted and to spend time with some girls. I met Sam Gravely Jr. that day. He was about three years older than I was and a native of Richmond, Virginia, who was on the UCLA campus training in the Navy's V-12 program—that branch's equivalent of the ASTP. Sam later began his seagoing career as a sailor aboard a submarine chaser that was one of only two World War II ships with a largely Negro crew. During thirty-eight years in the navy, Sam achieved many firsts: the first Negro to command a U.S. Navy warship, the first to command an American warship under combat conditions, the first Negro admiral, the first Negro vice admiral, and the first Negro to command a U.S. fleet.

My single day at UCLA was memorable for more than my brief encounter with Sam Gravely. That day I was looking for one young lady in particular, but she was not to be found. I met another very good-looking girl, Philippa Jones, near the student commons and learned that she lived in north Pasadena down the street from Jackie Robinson. (In 1949, she introduced me to Jackie when he spotted her in the stands at a Brooklyn Dodgers–Chicago Cubs game at Wrigley Field in Chicago and came over to say hello.) I drove her home that day and told her I would soon be shipping out. I asked that she answer my letters from overseas, and she said she would. The next morning I headed back to Arizona. Although I wrote her only a few letters during my term of service overseas, Philippa and I married two years later and have been married for sixty-two years.

Not long after I returned from my brief furlough, Combat Team 370, more than four thousand men, boarded trains and headed east. We were not informed of our destination. Again we stopped twice a day at isolated sidings to exercise. One day we ran through the streets of Knoxville, Tennessee, stripped down to our undershirts, and then headed right back to the train.

Eventually we reached our destination, Camp Patrick Henry in Hampton Roads, Virginia, which was to become our port of embarkation. There we learned how to climb down ropes from a sinking ship. We marched around the camp and encountered German prisoners of war marching in their gray uniforms. They were quite disciplined and sang German songs and counted off in German as we passed. We, of course, straightened up as soon as we saw them and counted off much louder, "Ain't no use in goin' home, Jody got your gal and gone, hut, two, three, fo," drowning out the Germans. I could sense no reaction from the Germans as they watched a unit of American Negro troops.

Several of us, including Lane Warren of Texas, had our hair either cut off entirely or shaved in the manner of a Mohawk

Indian. We wanted to look fierce when we went into combat. Warren was probably only sixteen, a slightly built kid who had lied about his age in order to get into the army and into combat. He liked anything dangerous, and he liked to shoot. At Ft. Huachuca he spent time in the stockade for taking a playful shot at the commanding officer of L Company. He was freed when the battalion was sent overseas.

A few of us headed off one day to visit Hampton Institute, a nearby Negro college. We were supposed to sit in the back of the streetcar but ignored that bit of segregation.

I was promoted to the rank of private first class just before we left Fort Huachuca. An order came down from battalion or regimental headquarters through the company commander, listing all those soldiers who had been promoted. In addition to privates, the list would show who had become corporal, sergeant, staff sergeant, etc. As a private first class, I believe I earned somewhere around $60 a month.

Seixas, Chapell, and other ASTP fellows I had started out with in the 92nd had all been moved into different units. The men I was closest to now were other members of the S-2 Intelligence Squad and our operations sergeant, T. T. Davis. As I have indicated, Davis is the man largely responsible for the daily journal entries that form the core of this book. All of us were in Battalion Headquarters Company, and we were in the Battalion Headquarters Platoon. We were also friendly with other former ASTP soldiers in our battalion.

It was only after the war I learned that Emmett Chapell had been wounded in action and Barry Seixas killed on April 4, 1945, just one month before the war ended. Barry was from Berkeley, and when I returned to the university to complete my education, his mother invited me to dinner. It was very uncomfortable listening to her reminisce about Barry and ask questions that I did not want to answer about what war had been like. Barry is buried at the U.S. military cemetery in Florence, Italy. I visited his grave in 2002 while traveling with a group from the Archdiocese of Los Angeles and my son, Ivan A. Houston.

Early on the morning of July 15, 1944, Combat Team 370 lined the streets of Camp Patrick Henry. Each man answered to his name and number. We shouldered our packs and headed off to the train that would take us to our ship. Amidst all the joking and griping, I sensed a lot of heavy hearts. Personally I was ready to move on to the next phase of army duty.

The troops were quickly boarded and given sandwiches. Soon the train was racing through the outskirts of Norfolk, Virginia, and some of us longed to be in the comfortable little cottages we saw along the right-of-way. Some men from Virginia were able to identify the homes of relatives and friends they were leaving behind. In no time at all, we were at the port and going through another lineup, another roll call, complaining that we needed more hands to carry our duffel bags, full field packs, weapons, and the doughnuts being given us by the women of the Red Cross.

We staggered up the gangplank of the *USS Mariposa* at Hampton Roads, Virginia, under our heavy burdens, and more than four thousand men entered a new world. To many of us it was our first time aboard a ship of any kind, let alone a converted cruise ship. All of us wanted to explore the area, and so we wandered as far as the crowd and restrictions would permit.

With others in 3rd Battalion headquarters I was assigned to a small stateroom. There were twelve of us in the room, with four-tiered canvas bunks rising from floor to ceiling along three walls. We had a toilet and a bathtub. All water came from the ocean. If you wanted to wash, shave, or take a bath, you did it with cold salty water. Our platoon leader assigned the bunks so that there could be little or no bitching over who got which position.

We somehow thought we were going to return to camp; but after the last man in the regiment had boarded the ship, the tugs began working the liner out into a murky sea. It was 12:15 PM Eastern Standard Time, July 15, 1944. I was truly surprised that we were on our way across the ocean since we had been led to believe that this was just going to be a practice run. Within two hours the *Mariposa* was in open sea, and light showers that had marked our departure had changed to a driving rain slanting against a leaden sky. The going became rough enough that a number of men were forced to the rail for more than a last glimpse of the fading shoreline. I hunkered down in my bunk and slept, read, and talked to my eleven roommates.

When night came, I went up on deck. It was completely dark, not a single light showing. I could see every star in the sky and the brilliant phosphorescence as the bow of our ship broke the water. It looked like fire. It was extraordinarily beautiful and filled me with awe. The next morning the sun rose above a calm sea. We were heading eastward with nothing but the foaming wake to break the monotony. Where was the convoy? Didn't all troopships travel in convoys for mutual protection? Weren't we vulnerable to sea and air attack? Those questions were on everyone's minds as conjecture and rumor passed from lip to lip. The wildest possibilities were bandied about. Only after some of the more grounded soldiers had approached members of the crew did we learn that the *Mariposa* was a converted speedy Matson luxury liner. We were told it had such great speed and maneuverability that it never traveled in convoy except in the most dangerous waters, and it had made many ocean crossings without loss of a single man. They told us the *Mariposa* was fast enough to outrun German submarines. Many men of the 3rd Battalion would have appreciated a few companion ships as reassurance and to break the broad expanse of water and sky, but others appreciated the speed achieved by traveling alone.

We were heading east but still had no idea precisely where we were going, whether through the Mediterranean or on to the China-Burma-India theater of war, where my brother Norman was serving in the quartermaster corps, driving trucks over The Hump from India to China.

The crossing must have been like thousands of other troopship crossings, the hours filled with washing down the decks, shopping in the ship's PX, boat drill, taking typhus shots, atabrine tablets to build resistance to malaria, undergoing periodic short-arm inspections, sweating out the long mess line that led into the merciless heat of the ship's belly, trying to find a comfortable spot on deck, and watching for the signal to darken the ship.

On our third night out, a great number of us became dreadfully ill. Retching soldiers bent by abdominal pain crawled to sick bay begging for relief. The medics worked throughout the night trying to ease their suffering. I spent the night moving between my bunk and the head but recovered fairly quickly. The sea was very calm throughout that period and the direct cause of the epidemic was not discovered, but steps were taken to prevent its recurrence. The PX halted all candy sales. We were lectured on the care of our mess equipment, and a bland diet was ordered for all hands. That last measure met with bitter complaint, especially by those who had not become ill. Everything soon returned to normal, but none of us will ever forget that miserable night.

Much of my time was spent with other ASTP members of the battalion. Jim Tucker was, like me, an intelligence scout observer in Headquarters Company. He was over six feet tall and proud of his athletic ability. After the war Tucker became a noted economist and vice president of the Federal Reserve Bank of Richmond, Virginia. McKinley B. Scott, George Gray, and Sergeant James E. Reid were from I Company. Scott was a handsome guy and a baseball player. Gray was an impressive hulk with the look of an Indian chief. Reid, older than the rest of us, wore glasses and was our informal leader. We played bridge together and watched the ship roll over the waves. Tucker and I survived the war; Scott, Gray, and Reid were all killed within four months of our landing in Italy.

One event that never failed to arouse a great deal of interest was the daily antiaircraft gun drill held by the ship's crew. We viewed the winging of toy balloons with professional and personal interest, and observing the crew's proficiency increased our confidence. As we moved across the Atlantic, there was constant discussion of our ultimate destination. Africa, England, Italy, and the Pacific were all mentioned as possibilities. Our course continued eastward, but the zigzag tactics of the ship often confused us. Constant advances in time were further evidence that we must be traveling almost due east.

Seven days after leaving Virginia, the *Mariposa*—with beautiful precision—joined a huge convoy. More ships than most of us had ever seen at one time steamed along on all sides. It was a thrilling and comforting sight. Then, on July 23, we heard the welcome cry, "Land!" and everyone strained to pick out the misty form ahead. It was the coast of Africa. Most of us were looking for jungle since the only perception we had of that continent came from Tarzan movies. As we plowed on, another great shadowy mass took definite shape. The mighty Rock of Gibraltar towered above us as we steamed by. We were picked up by an escort of American destroyers. Books and musical instruments were laid aside and card games stopped while all of us studied the ever-changing shores of Gibraltar on our left and Africa—the land of our ancestors—on the starboard side. We were aware, all of us, that our forebears had been brought from here to America forcibly in chains and that because of slavery we remained second-class citizens. Yet, despite that bitter history, we were committed to fight for America against the evil of Nazi Germany. Land looked mighty good to us, even if it resembled the area of the Huachuca mountains at our home base.

On July 24 the *Mariposa* sailed past several French warships flying the tricolor and docked in the port of Oran, Algeria, at 0700, five hours in advance of Eastern Standard Time. We had crossed the Atlantic and part of the Mediterranean in nine days, excellent even by peacetime standards.

Before long it was evident that we would leave the *Mariposa*. All equipment was gathered, and once again we struggled with our unwieldy duffel bags while sweating under the African sun and moving on legs unsteady from lack of activity. The soldiers laboring on the dock as we disembarked were American Negroes who yelled that we would soon be doing the same labor as they were. Most of them had come from combat units that had been converted to labor battalions. The 9th and 10th Cavalry, the original Buffalo Soldiers, had been sent to North Africa in March 1944, inactivated, and returned as service troops.

Little time passed before we boarded another ship, the *George C. Squire*, a trim and clean navy transport that was terribly overcrowded. It was governed by navy discipline. The enlisted men of our battalion were bunked at the very bottom of the ship. A cargo hole was right above us, and ammunition was loaded after we had settled into our places. One slip in the loading process, and we would have been history. Over the next three days, we practiced getting out from under the hole and up onto the deck. We learned how to abandon ship if hit by a German submarine. When the *George C. Squire* weighed anchor on July 26, we all would have given a great deal to be back on the *Mariposa*.

While complaining of our discomforts and trying to organize a cup of ice cream from the ship's store—"For Navy Personnel Only"—we still had time to search for clues to our ultimate destination. Once the convoy settled into a steady north-northeast course, everyone began trying to remember all they knew about Italy—"Land of the Boot"—and the war there. I had kept up with the war and knew that the 15th Army Group, headed by Britain's Field Marshal Harold Alexander and comprising the U.S. Fifth Army under General Mark Clark and the British Eighth Army under Field Marshal Bernard Montgomery, had invaded Italy in September 1943; and after a series of heavy losses at Salerno, Cassino, and Anzio, the 15th had liberated Rome on June 4, 1944, less than two months before. The Allied armies had sprinted north to the Arno River line. Battle in Italy had been extremely difficult because the obstructive Apennine mountains ran the length of the Boot—and because the Nazis had placed their greatest defensive general, "Smiling Albert" Kesselring, in command of their 10th and 14th armies in northern Italy.

As the *Squire* turned directly north, officers started passing out little booklets on how to speak Italian. We discussed the war in Italy. Despite the statements made to us by all commanders, many men refused to believe that we were actually going to be sent into combat. Those who argued that we would eventually form a labor battalion pinned part of their argument on the fact that a number of cases labeled "Shovels" had been loaded onto the ship.

The *Squire* sailed past a smoking mountain: it was Vesuvius, the volcano that had destroyed Pompeii in 79 A.D. It had erupted in March 1944 for the first time in four hundred years, and the live volcano welcomed us to the shell-torn port of Naples, about 275 miles south of our army's front line along the Arno River. The harbor was littered with sunken ships, scuttled by the Germans as they were pushed north. Army engineers built a causeway across some of the sunken ships, and we carried, pulled, rolled, or dragged our duffel bags to trucks waiting in the port. The cases labeled "Shovels" were left behind.

On Sunday, July 30, as dusk was just creeping over the smelly, littered streets of Naples, we disembarked. Hargrove reports that our arrival was heralded by wild cheering from Negro service troops on the dock, but I remember no cheering. However, I do clearly remember that urchins were begging everywhere, and accompanying the roar of trucks carrying the materials of war was the clatter of horse-drawn vehicles and the whine of a multitude of adult beggars pleading for food in the fetid air. They snatched any article not tied down. Trying to chase them down the darkening streets was useless. All along the line young girls were offering themselves to the soldiers for soap or cigarettes. To men who had seen no women for two weeks, officers and enlisted men alike, the women were a great temptation, but we moved on and soon arrived by truck at Naples's main train station. At the staging area, Lieutenant General Jacob Devers, commanding general of United States forces in the Mediterranean theater of operations, commended the combat team for its discipline and fine appearance.

We sat on the cool pavement until a long electric train arrived with a cacophony of bells and whistles. The troops squeezed into the uncomfortable coaches and the train started up, soon hurtling through a series of tunnels before arriving at Bagnoli, a western seaside suburb of Naples. There we waited, almost asleep on our feet, for the rest of the battalion to arrive on the next train. Captain Price, our operations officer, led us on foot up a winding road toward some attractive buildings that we thought for a time were to be our quarters. No such luck. We continued on tired feet up an apparently endless dusty road through cool vineyards. The climb ended at a castlelike structure where a foreign guard challenged us before allowing us to pass through a large gate. We moved through the darkness down a steep, rough trail. When we reached bottom, we continued along hard road, ready to drop, until someone said, "Your area is over to the left." Few took time to pitch tents. We simply flopped down and were soon asleep on the ground.

Morning revealed our location to be a wooded area surrounded by steep hills. It was like being inside a large dust bowl. The soil was so powdery that a cloud was raised with each step. The area was referred to as "The Crater" and was probably the site of an extinct volcano. Some of the truck drivers from the port battalion told us that the King of Italy had once used the area as a hunting ground. Setting up camp was the first priority. Some downed a can of C-rations before setting off to work. Combating the dust was quite a problem, but we found that the principles we had learned in Louisiana and Arizona worked just as well in Italy. Our neighbors, however, were a surprise. We learned that the hearty young men in purple trunks pounding past our camp on bare feet were members of the Brazilian Expeditionary Force. We saw immediately that the Portuguese-speaking Brazilians were integrated, black and white moving along together. That was a revelation. We also saw many-starred soldiers in green uniforms, who were partisan Italians fighting with the Allies. We admired the Italians' ability to carry with ease a pack that resembled our duffel bags. Later we grew suspicious when we noticed that our duffel bags had begun to disappear.

In the next few days, we climbed the dusty, steep sides of the camp and did conditioning exercises and guard duty. There was no space for athletic activity because of the nature of the terrain and the number of other camps in the vicinity. When we received word that the quarantine we were under as newly arrived troops had been lifted, we were overjoyed. Some passes were issued, and those fortunate to receive one were eager to see what could be had with the unfamiliar Allied currency and the few phrases of Italian we had picked up.

General Mark Clark visited the 370th Combat Team on August 8. I saw him more than once during my tour of duty, when he appeared to be doing a general inspection. I never saw Winston Churchill, though I understand that he visited the headquarters of Combat Team 370 around the time we were preparing to go into battle. Churchill was the Allies' leader largely responsible for the invasion of Italy. He favored a strategy of attacking Germany from the south rather than from across the English Channel.

After a few nights in the crater, we were sharply reminded of the purpose that had brought us there. At 0200 one morning, the entire camp was awakened by a series of explosions and stuttering *ack-ack* (antiaircraft fire). The rim of the crater was roofed by tracer bullets that made brilliant patterns in the night. Some men began digging foxholes; others just hugged the ground waiting for the worst. Nothing happened, but the explosions made us realize that this was no exercise; we were very close to the war, and this was for keeps. The Germans had bombed the port of Naples.

Three days later, the advance party from our combat team left for the front. Many wanted to go, but only Colonel Daugette and a few officers and men from each company were selected. The rest of us continued to hike up and down around the crater, read *Stars and Stripes*, practice our Italian, and have the cobblers on the hill fasten leather tops to our shoes so that they would look like combat boots. It was not long before we had the real boots.

August 10 brought an end to this as the 3rd Battalion left by truck for Naples. The rest of the day and far into the night we idled on the dock, waiting to board the *John Jay*. It was twenty-four hours later that we finally weighed anchor and sailed northward. The trip on the filthy, overcrowded ship, eating C-rations when we were able and sleeping in the rain on the messy deck, was a most disagreeable experience. Fortunately, it only lasted two days, and on August 12 at 1140 hours we landed at Civitavecchia, the battered port forty miles north of Rome on the Tyrrhenian

Sea. The rest of the combat team came north to Civitavecchia by army truck. We were now 125 miles south of the front lines. At Civitavecchia we discovered that several of the Port Battalion Service (PBS) truck drivers were former members of the 3rd Battalion. It made the country seem a little less strange and the war a little less terrible when we were able to talk with someone who had experienced several months of battle unscathed.

We made formal camp about four miles north of Civitavecchia on a plain that sloped gently toward the sea. The engineers hung lister bags—canvas containers for water about six feet long—on tripods. The water was treated, but not tasty; the GIs used it to fill their canteens. Early during our stay there, we found a well near our camp and used a bucket to draw fresh water. I remember it being some of the best water I had ever tasted. One evening at camp, when we were having canned peaches for dessert, I was attacked by a swarm of yellow jackets and was stung on the tongue. I actually bit one before spitting it out.

Parked on a railroad track near our camp was a huge, destroyed German artillery gun. It was Anzio Annie, the giant gun that had been fired at the Anzio beachhead from a position near Rome.

We began a training schedule that included, along with the usual subjects, swimming in the Tyrrhenian Sea about four miles away, developing our rifle marksmanship, and getting an orientation on the progress of the war. Some of this progress we could see firsthand.

Early on the morning of August 15, we were awakened by a dull roar in the sky. Dawn revealed hundreds of planes, C-47s with gliders attached, speeding northeast. The parade of air power continued well into the afternoon, and we knew that we were watching history being made even before news of the invasion of southern France—Operation Dragoon, between Toulon and Cannes—reached us through the pages of *Stars and Stripes*. The military newspaper arrived about once a week; it came down from higher headquarters through regimental and battalion headquarters to the companies. There was a copy for everyone.

At Civitavecchia, Captain and company commander Hugh D. Shires called me in and told me that he was naming me the battalion clerk. I became a Technician Fifth Grade and was called Corporal Houston. That meant another $10 a month or so. The army wanted us to buy war bonds, so every month that I was in the army, regardless of my pay, I would have a payroll deduction to buy some denomination of bond. In my new position I would report directly to Battalion Sergeant Major Norwood Boyette of New York, who in turn reported to Captain Shires. Ranking above Shires was Colonel Daugette, and above him was our regimental commander, Colonel Sherman.

As battalion clerk I carried out orders from Captain Shires, First Sergeant Ross, and Operations Sergeant T. T. Davis. I often received and gave information directly to Colonel Daugette and the other battalion staff officers. All written orders from Daugette, Colonel Sherman, or even General Almond that were meant for the men of the 3rd Battalion went through me. I typed some and distributed others. I had learned to type when I was in the eighth grade. It was one of the most useful courses I have ever taken. I was at the hub of activities and generally knew what was going on. Though Sergeant Major Boyette was my immediate superior, and the chief administrative noncommissioned officer of the battalion, the only time I ever saw him after we got on line—entered combat—was when we were pulled back to a rear area. He spent most of his time at a rear-echelon headquarters or at division headquarters in Viareggio. Boyette was a slight person, a very good administrator, and a lightning typist. He was from New York and often talked about how much he missed his wife. He was about thirty years old.

At Civitavecchia we prepared for the day when we would be ordered into the combat line. Weapons were checked, final issues of clothing made, and vehicles uncrated and assembled. They included not only trucks but Ducks, amphibious vehicles that could carry troops across terrain and also ford a river. They had wheels and a rounded boatlike bottom. The Ducks were not intended for our use, however; they were headed off for service in France.

When Major Sturdevant, executive officer, acting for Colonel Daugette, received the order from regimental headquarters to join Combat Command A of the 1st Armored Division ("Old Ironsides"), to which the 370th Combat Team was attached, everything was just about set. On August 22, 1944, 3rd Battalion 370th Combat Team, the first unit of the 92nd Division to get a combat assignment, broke camp at Civitavecchia and embarked for Cenaia, 120 miles north and just behind the Arno River line.

The convoy to Cenaia was essentially no different from other convoys that had transported us from one place to another. However, it was night, and blackout lights were used. I traveled in one of the army trucks. We sat about eight men to the side as our drivers—most drivers were in the Quartermaster Corps and were Negro soldiers—got us to our next location. But on this journey there was a great deal of difference in the way we gripped our weapons, and the tense feeling in our stomach muscles told us that something was unusual. As darkness settled over us on the convoy headed northward, everyone was very anxious that the leading vehicle take the right direction. The column finally halted, and the call for blackout was passed along the line. In the cool still blackness that followed, we could hear for the first time the dull, distant thud of artillery. An involuntary shudder shook many a spine.

The convoy continued until it had negotiated several steep hills and wound into a thick grove of trees. In the darkness it was difficult to determine the nature of our location, but each company was given an area in which to sleep. The order was to pitch no tents but instead to dig slit trenches. The last part of that order needed no repetition because every man was soon earnestly at work. We thought we were going to have to dig foxholes; but instead, we of Headquarters Platoon, about thirty men, were installed in an abandoned villa, where we slept on a floor that was either tile or concrete. We wrapped our bodies in our blankets and used our helmets as pillows. We were so tired that comfort did not matter.

About this time, before we moved up toward the front line, two GIs were brought into headquarters along with a male civilian. They were being charged with rape. I never saw the woman, and all I knew was that the men were being sent back for court-martial. That was the only time I ever saw Colonel Daugette become livid with anger. Other than that single episode, I was unaware of any charges of rape during the balance of my service in Italy. I never learned what happened to the alleged rapists.

The villa that became our initial headquarters, and those dwellings that succeeded it during our tenure in Italy, were abandoned, except for an occasional resident old gentleman. The only women we saw were old, too, and they invariably tried to get the leavings of our mess, begging us regularly to empty everything, even any leftover coffee, into one pail. Young women were nowhere to be seen, and most young men were off serving with the Italian partisans or had been carried off by the Germans to work in labor gangs.

In camp and in barracks, before we entered combat, all latrines were wide open, as many as twenty places in a row. Soldiers socialized while doing their thing. Each latrine on the line was about eight to ten feet long, a foot wide, and about two feet deep, dug out of sight of German observation posts. A pile of dirt with a shovel was kept alongside the latrine. The shovel and dirt were used to cover up any leavings. Officers had their own area. In combat zones soldiers from the Ammunition and Pioneer (A&P) platoon dug latrines for those of us at battalion headquarters. Members of the A&P, in addition to digging, carried ammunition to the battle zones.

Getting caught using the latrine during a heavy shelling was quite exciting. Those were the formal arrangements, but anyone could "let their load beside the road and go on quite contented." In the rear areas, the army built giant outhouses, used them for a while, covered them up with lye and dirt, and then moved on. It was not until we reached Barga, months later, that I saw my first Italian toilet: no seat, just a hole in the concrete floor and two places for your feet. Those dug by our A&P Platoon were not much worse. I remember the urinals in Florence. They were placed in the outside walls of many buildings. Women's toilets were usually in the middle of a road or street, screened off on either side. Toilets were one manifestation of a different culture.

On August 23, 1944, some of the advance party posed questions concerning conditions in the line. Colonel Daugette took the staff and company commanders to the command post of the 14th Armored Infantry Battalion for orientation and to the various command posts that we would subsequently occupy in relief of that battalion. The closer we drove to the front, the more unreal the situation seemed. The battalion command post was set up in a bright little community seemingly untouched by the war. Civilians walked around at will, begging in the garrison-like chow line for handouts. The total absence of foxholes made us a little self-conscious about our frantic entrenching of the night before some ten miles back.

The courteous, efficient, battle-wise veterans of the all-White 1st Armored Division soon put us at ease and began teaching us the rudiments of war. They assured us that good, strong, well-protected houses made excellent command posts, even for front-line units, and were to be used whenever possible. They also told us that it seemed very quiet now, but any careless exposure of personnel or vehicles would bring down a rain of artillery fire from the ever-watchful Germans. They gave us maps and overlays and pointed out positions, explaining everything carefully and in detail, until the jigsaw puzzle became a clear picture. The overlays were created on clear acetate film and showed our positions and the Germans' positions, which had been identified by our intelligence unit.

As we made final preparations for combat, the 3rd Battalion was assigned the code name Blue. First Battalion was Red, and 2nd Battalion was White. Regiment was referred to as Ditto. Thus, when Ditto Blue was called for, it meant 3rd Battalion, 370th Infantry. All of this was designed to confuse the Germans if they intercepted any of our messages or telephone calls.

The Allied line along the Arno River had been static for some time, with the 1st Armored Division responsible for a twenty-two-kilometer sector running from Cascina to the Evola river. The 1st Armored Division, which had been on the run from Rome all the way to the banks of the Arno, comprised mostly tanks, accompanied by some armored infantry. Later, when action was in or near the Apennines, the tanks could not advance because of the hilly terrain so the 92nd replaced them.

To the right of the 1st Armored was the hard-fighting Sixth South African Division; on the left was Task Force 45. Combat Command A under Colonel Howze, composed of the 14th Armored Infantry Battalion, elements of the 81st Cavalry Reconnaissance Squadron, and the 1st Tank Battalion, had been holding the left flank of the 1st Armored sector. Combat Command A's role was to maintain contact with Task Force 45 on the left and the 11th Armored Infantry Battalion on the right.

Because of the continued threat of a German counteroffensive, a plan of defense was established. It consisted of a series of outposts stretching more than thirty miles along the south bank of the Arno, supported by machine guns and mortars organized in depth. A strong motorized patrol tied the inner defenses together while a large reserve held prepared positions on the high ground about seven kilometers from the Arno. The 68th Field Artillery Battalion and the Armored Group's (AG) 4th Tank Battalion were in general support. The 91st Field Artillery Battalion and the AG's 1st Tank Battalion were in direct support. From battalion headquarters, our head of battalion operations went to higher headquarters and talked with the various staff members there, who were just as helpful and unassuming as the other members of the 1st Armored Division had been. We learned that our 3rd Battalion would relieve the 14th Armored Infantry Battalion at dark on August 23. Relief would include elements of the 81st Reconnaissance Battalion, who were working with the 14th Armored Infantry Battalion, giving us about a five-kilometer front along the winding Arno River, facing the elements of the Germans' 16th SS Panzergrenadier Reichsfuehrer Division, against whom we were to defend our sector of responsibility.

We were also to be responsible for maintenance of contact with Task Force 45 on our left and protection of the left flank of the 1st Armored Division on our right. My job was to remain in constant touch with battalion Intelligence (S-2), to record entries in the Journal (S-3), and to send casualty and strength information to regimental headquarters each night (S-1).

Our objective as the 370th Regimental Combat Team was to cross the Arno River and break through the Germans' Gothic Line, Field Marshal Kesselring's last major line of defense in northern Italy. The Gothic Line, built in 1943 by German engineers and Italian laborers, was north of the Arno River and stretched from La Spezia on the Ligurian Sea across the northern Apennines and the Serchio Valley to Pesaro on the Adriatic. It was a ten-mile-deep block of fortifications extending through the natural defensive wall of the northern Apennines, with crests and peaks that rose to seven thousand feet. Gothic Line emplacements included concrete-reinforced gun pits and trenches, more than two thousand machine-gun nests with interlocking fire, 479 antitank gun, mortar, and assault gun positions, 120,000 meters of barbed wire, minefields, and miles of antitank ditches.

It was quite an assignment for a green unit, and we went to work with extra pains to see that every detail of the relief would meet the standards of the veteran outfits we would be working with. Transportation, ammunition, rations, maps, overlays, guides, and instructions were checked and double-checked until everything seemed ready.

A forward command post, consisting of the commanding officer, the executive officer, and S-3 and S-2 sections, operations and intelligence, respectively, were moved from the old house we had been occupying to a larger structure, Villa Remaggi, and Sections 1 and 4, adjutant and supply, respectively, set up several miles back from battalion headquarters. I moved with the forward command post. We were in place and functioning by the time the troops began moving up at dusk. The move to the front through small villages was quite emotional. The Italians knew we were going to fight the dreaded Germans and that some of us would not come back. They threw flowers at our vehicles. They handed flowers and wine to those of us riding in the vehicles. They threw kisses at us.

Villa Remaggi was a farm and vineyard along the south bank of the Arno. The grapes looked ready to pick. The residents of the villa had left, but there were a few chickens still roaming the farmyard. Our soldiers, most of whom were from America's rural South, caught the chickens and fried them in the bacon grease from our Ten-in-One ration packs. These differed from C- and K-rations in that they were designed to be used in advance of the arrival of field kitchens. Each case provided nonperishable food for ten men for one day and could be eaten either hot or cold. Five menus were offered, with each ration providing 4,100 calories. Each case also included cigarettes, water purification tablets, matches, salt, can openers, toilet paper, toilet soap, and paper towels. Cooking was done on small, portable gasoline-fueled stoves.

Headquarters Company and Company K, the reserve company, established command posts in the vicinity of the battalion command post. I was now in a frontline combat position. Officers and men would frequently come and go throughout the day, but most of the activity happened at night to avoid observation by the Germans across the Arno. We were always on guard, since we assumed that the Germans would send a combat patrol to test our positions. Machine-gun fire would be heard all the time. Artillery fire thundered near and far. At Villa Remaggi, two hundred to four hundred yards behind the front line, we created maps from frequent reports received by runner, telephone, and walkie-talkie. We did all our work, including mapping and all paperwork, without electricity. The villa was kept darkened so that no giveaway light would mark us as a target. The candles we used were tapers about a foot long. Company M, whose heavy weapon components were divided among the frontline companies, made its command post in a schoolhouse about 300 yards from battalion headquarters.

ITALY: The Beginning
July 30 - August 23, 1944

Florence

Cascina
August 23
Cenaia

LIGURIAN SEA

Civitavecchia
August 12   Rome

Naples
July 30

TYRRHENIAN SEA

MEDITERRANEAN SEA

IONIAN SEA

ENTRY INTO COMBAT: AUGUST 1944

On the night of August 23–24, 1944, as we prepared to enter combat, we suddenly realized that this was no training exercise: an enemy patrol might be lurking behind the next culvert or house, or the deafening roar of a firearm might be the next and last sound that we heard. The accidental clanking of our rifle against our steel helmet might be heard by every German in the area and would surely bring down a rain of fire.

Company I, under its commander, Lieutenant Jesse Jarman, on the left, with its command post at Cascina, reported enemy activity around an area designated Outpost 4. In the firing that followed, Platoon Sergeant James E. Reid of Company I, with whom I had played cards and passed idle hours only days before as we crossed the Atlantic, was wounded and later died, thus becoming the first fatality of the 3rd Battalion, the first battle casualty of the 92nd Division, and the first Negro in the European Theater of war to die in infantry combat. Just like that, someone I had known was gone. There was much confusion during our first night in combat. A password to be used each night was given to every member of the Fifth Army, but an American woman named Mildred Gillars, who broadcast German propaganda to the American troops each night as Axis Sally, also had the password somehow. Her revelations enabled the Germans to infiltrate American positions. Axis Sally was to play music for us every night—jazz—and if the Germans had taken any prisoners from our unit, she was certain to announce it. She would say things like, "Give up your arms," and "Why are you fighting?" We found her jabber entertaining, never demoralizing.

On that first night of combat, our units directed artillery fire at a German patrol as we saw it withdraw across the Arno River. The relief we provided continued without further casualties, although there was some returned artillery fire in Company L's sector. By 0615 on the morning of August 25, the battalion commander was able to report to the 1st Armored Division that the 14th Armored Infantry Battalion had officially been relieved, although a few of their men would remain with us until we were fully oriented.

When I woke up that morning, I looked out from a concealed position at the 3rd Battalion observation post and saw the Leaning Tower of Pisa. It was northwest of our position on the Arno. There were six scout observers in the intelligence unit at battalion headquarters manning the observation post. I maintained continual contact with the intelligence squad, which now consisted of Lane Warren, Fortunatus Sweeney, Robert Turner, Zane Grey Phoenix, Jim Tucker, and Bob Simpson. Warren later transferred to L Company and became a very aggressive squad leader. He was replaced by a very "correct" soldier from Washington, D.C., Negro society, Lloyd Parker. Parker thought all of us were uncouth and lacked class. He would categorize each soldier working around battalion headquarters, including me, indicating their place in Negro society. He also used to talk about high-society Negroes, whom he called "the muckety-muck." He was so proper and infuriating that we all had a good laugh at his rantings. He was truly a rare person. I managed somehow to get along with Parker, probably because I had been a student at the University of California. I should clarify that many times the guys in S-2, including me, would purposely use bad English and slang with a Southern accent because we did not want to appear too different from the semiliterate and illiterate soldiers we worked with. The use of dialect somehow stayed with me for several years after the war, and when I went to graduate school in Canada in 1948, some of the Canadian students thought I was from a Southern state.

The 370th Regimental Combat Team's immediate objective, ordered by the Fifth Army, was to cross the Arno and capture Mount Pisano, three miles wide and six miles long, lying north to south.

The first day of combat continued with sporadic exchanges of artillery fire. Later, enemy activity was observed on the north bank of the Arno and engaged with 81-mm mortar shells fired by the M Company mortar platoon led by Lieutenant Harry Cox. Lieutenant Cox, almost six feet five inches tall, was from San Mateo, California. He had the reputation of being able to put a mortar shell in your pocket from five hundred yards away. As darkness fell, one outpost after another experienced enemy shelling. A Lieutenant Phoenix (not Zane Grey) of M Company was wounded at Outpost 7. During our early days of combat, several other casualties were reported. Most of them were in Company L and were inflicted by our own men. Two of the victims were from the 1st Armored Division, adding complications to the change in command that was taking place. An inquiry was conducted by the Regimental S-2, and all units were warned against becoming trigger-happy.

Troop activities slowly began to slip into the routine of hourly reports to higher headquarters, distribution of rations, contacts with friendly units, and the questioning of suspicious civilians—all without slackening the constant watch for enemy activity. On August 26, the battalion's rifle companies I, K, and L were busy patrolling. Lieutenant Reuben L. Horner of Company L and seven men of Company I under Lieutenant Isaac Jones scouted the Arno in our zone for possible crossing sites and signs of enemy movement. The patrol was successful in both endeavors—discovering a safe place to cross and observing two enemy patrols of superior force, against which ambushes were later planned.

At the time, Lieutenant Horner was in his early thirties. He became the most decorated officer in our battalion, and before his army career ended—nineteen years later, in 1963—he had won the Distinguished Service Medal, the Silver Star with oak leaf cluster, the Bronze Star with four clusters, and three Purple Hearts. He retired as a colonel. He died only a few years ago. I did not know Lieutenant Horner personally; none of the officers fraternized with enlisted men like me. However, I did have many opportunities to observe how he operated. He was intelligent, brave, and a leader. Like most of the other Negro officers, he was not subservient when talking to White officers of superior rank. Horner was from Tucson, Arizona.

In my position, I had no traffic with any of the company commanders. I saw them come and go, heard them speak, give orders, and take orders from the colonel. I was just another GI, working in and around headquarters. I remained busy in the sprawling villa occupied by battalion headquarters, often recording hourly and daily activities in the operations journal and frequently typing copies of the journal, which would be sent to regimental headquarters. Other parts of battalion headquarters were staffed by a message center that handled the runners from each company and the telephone lines that were connected to each company's headquarters. Radio contact was available but used infrequently. Soldiers in the communications platoon carried large spools of telephone wire all over the front lines. The wire was heavy and broken frequently by accident or by enemy artillery fire. By code I also reported the numbers killed in action (KIA), wounded in action (WIA), or missing in action (MIA) to regimental headquarters each evening by telephone. The only guys I would chew the fat with were the men in my section, whom I was working with all the time. I would talk to Sergeant Davis and Sergeant Ross. On occasion I would speak with Captain Shires, because I worked with him daily, and with our S-2 intelligence guys. But there was none of the "brother" talk you might find among Black men of different strata on the streets of any city in America. It's common in the Negro community to do that, but certainly not so in the army. The soldiers adhered to the hierarchy of the command structure. Among the enlisted men, the most commonly used word was "motherfucker." However, it was not used in an insulting way. One White officer grew quite upset at hearing it over and over again and asked me why the men used that word. I told him that I honestly did not know. Looking back, I realize that the men using the word with overwhelming frequency had limited vocabularies and the word served a multitude of purposes in their communication.

The next night we learned from the regimental supply officer that only a small quantity of 81-mm mortar ammunition was available to us because the 3rd Battalion had somehow not been included in August's ammo allocation. We had been limited to two hundred rounds given us by the 1st Armored Division.

Ambush and reconnaissance patrols went scouting but without success. While they were out, another type of activity was taking place overhead. A Jerry observation plane, popularly known as "Bed-Check Charley," swooped out of the moonlit sky and dropped five or six antipersonnel bombs on and near the battalion outpost, slightly injuring eight men. Although we had heard Charley before, we had believed his chief purpose to be the identification of possible artillery targets, but now the lazy hum of his engine brought a feeling of apprehension to all who were on the road. And it ensured added care that our blackout was complete before candles were lighted.

We remained at Villa Remaggi, amid the vineyards and farms of the Arno River Valley, for about one week. (Weeks later, after we had moved up into the Serchio River Valley near the medieval Tuscan town of Barga, we moved our headquarters almost every night. Our intelligence unit worked with the Italian partisans and chose the spot for our night's headquarters.) Though I had originally been a member of the S-2 squad, I was now working with S-1, the adjutant, and with S-3, complementing the work of Operations Sergeant T. T. Davis, creating maps and reports. We continued to do our work by candlelight.

Enemy activity increased. Artillery fire was especially heavy in Cascina, and all outposts reported instances of enemy infiltration and wiretapping. We met those threats with more patrols. The artillery supporting our infantry used Piper Cub aircraft to spot enemy positions. On August 29, Lieutenant Horner led a raiding party consisting of thirty men—mostly of Company L and armed with machine guns, submachine guns, grenades, and bazookas—and set out to invade the north bank of the Arno. It was near midnight, and there was a brilliant moon. The raid was well planned and called for close artillery support and radio and telephone communication with the rear. After the initial concentration of fire by the 598th Field Artillery, Lieutenant Horner and two men, Sergeant Hicks of Company L and Private Lane Warren of our S-2, followed by sixteen others, waded into the chilly waters of the Arno and began to search the north bank for enemy. They were the first men in our battalion to cross the Arno. Emplacements and other evidence of recent occupation were found, but the Jerries had probably withdrawn because of the artillery fire. The mission was accomplished at 0130, and the party returned to their respective platoon areas. Headquarters was pleased to learn that a definite crossing had been established, and requested minute details of the operation. Sergeant Hicks of Company L was an outstanding platoon sergeant. He was a leader among the enlisted men and the noncommissioned officers and had been awarded the Expert Infantryman's Badge while still at Fort Huachuca. Later he would be given a combat commission for his actions on line, and it was as Lieutenant Hicks that he was killed in action.

On the night of August 30, Company K, under Captain Reedy, relieved Jarman's Company I. Reedy was the only White commanding officer among our four line companies. I did not know of his abilities. He did not seem very loquacious but did appear calm under fire. Some of his platoon leaders were also White. No White officer reported to a Negro company commander. This system assured that the best officer was not always in charge.

The last day of August 1944 began with a GI running for cover into the command post yard and being shot in the eye by one of our own. As the day unfolded, particularly heavy artillery fire from the north and northeast was harassing our installations all along the entire front and knocking out our telephone lines. This, plus a prisoner of war report stating that only one rifle company of seventy men and a heavy weapons company were holding the line opposite us, made repeated talk of an enemy withdrawal highly credible, and it gave added importance to the reconnaissance in force planned for the night. Lieutenant Bentley and a small group reconnoitered for crossing sites in that sector. None was located, but the patrol drew enemy machine-gun fire that established their continued presence. A patrol consisting of men from Company L and Company M also drew mortar and machine-gun fire in the right sector. In spite of rumors to the contrary, Jerry had not withdrawn.

The Germans were using what was called a burp gun, the MP-38 submachine gun, later replaced by the MP-40. It held thirty-two rounds and could fire five hundred rounds a minute. When we heard that quick repetitive burping sound, we knew that the Germans were within four hundred yards or less. It seemed like every German soldier had a burp gun. I'm not certain that was so, but they were everywhere. With our semiautomatic M-1s, we could fire only one round at a time from a clip of eight. The German soldier could fire many rounds in the same instant. We were clearly outgunned.

We did have .30-caliber light machine guns, which were air-cooled, as a part of the weapons platoon of each rifle company. Our heavy machine guns were .50 caliber and water-cooled, but they were only in M Company, the heavy weapons company of the 3rd Battalion. Both kinds of machine guns were used on tripods.

The fully automatic weapon that rifle companies carried was the BAR—Browning Automatic Rifle. It was a .30-caliber air-cooled weapon that weighed more than fifteen pounds and could fire as many as 650 rounds a minute.

Company I, while in reserve on August 31, had been carefully briefed on the situation and was to enter the action: A party would cross the river north of Cascina and clean out an area about six hundred yards square to include the town of Lugnano. Two platoons would advance abreast as soon as possible thereafter, and one would remain in reserve in a bridgehead position on the north bank. A platoon of Company K would support from the south bank and cover the withdrawal of Company I. Aid men and an A&P Squad from Headquarters Company were to operate with Company I. The 598th and 91st Field Artillery Battalions and one section of Company M's 81-mm mortars would support the operation with planned fire.

I asked Lieutenant Harrington, the intelligence officer (and one of only four Negro officers in the headquarters group) if I could cross the Arno with Company I. Harrington refused to let me go. (The other Negro officers were Lieutenant Oxley, S-4, supplies, Lieutenant Brown, antitank platoon, and Lieutenant Carter, motor officer.) I was disappointed because I felt it would be a great adventure.

Three members of battalion intelligence went forward to aid the attack, and by 2340 hours everything was set and the signal given for the artillery preparation.

By 0050 on September 1 all of Company I was across the river, and a few moments later a green flare indicated that the forward platoons had reached their objectives in Lugnano, a village on the north bank, where the sound of exploding grenades and bursts of small-arms fire could be heard. No enemy was found in the ghostlike town, so the raiding party returned to the south bank of the Arno as had been planned, happy that there had been no casualties but somewhat disappointed they hadn't taken any prisoners. The 1st Armored Division was not disappointed at this negative report. We received orders to occupy positions on the north bank of the river at dawn and to be prepared to follow the enemy withdrawal. A platoon of Company L and a platoon of Company K occupied positions at Lugnano and nearby San Giovanni alla Vena, respectively, while the remainder of the battalion assembled at Cascina with full field equipment and rations. Company L had encountered a few snipers, but otherwise their movement across the Arno was without incident, and by noon on September 1, Companies K and I were moving to the northwest, combing the countryside for any Jerries who might have straggled. Company L was held in reserve.

Men, materiel, and supplies were being brought up to the Arno in a steady stream, and engineers were working on fords and bridges. Orders were coming in thick and fast. Before the first order could be executed, a second would come, changing it. By 1600 our troops were beyond Noce, three kilometers from Cascina, having searched every house for enemy before proceeding to Caprona. Just beyond Caprona it was expected that our battalion would contact the 100th Battalion, whose right flank rested on the edge of a small stream, but plans were changed when tanks of the 1st Armored Division found it necessary to go north to Calci in the high grounds of Mount Pisano, in order to bypass blown bridges and drive the occupying Germans away. Company L was to proceed to Calci by truck, and from there northwest to Asciano, where they would join Companies K and I.

Terence P. Rogers, one of the men who, like me, had begun his army experience in the ASTP, was killed by mortar fire when a shell hit him after we had crossed the Arno. A medic I was friendly with told me that he had been hit while in either a foxhole or shell hole.

The 100th Battalion, which we were not to be closely allied with in action until spring of 1945, was composed entirely of Japanese American volunteers from Hawaii. They had an outstanding combat record. They joined the 442nd Regimental Combat Team, also Japanese Americans, during fierce fighting in France and returned to Italy to fight as part of the 92nd Division in the last campaign of the war. The 442nd Combat Team became one of the military's most highly decorated units. When I first saw the troops of the 100th Battalion in 1944, they looked just like most of the Japanese students I had gone to high school with at Los Angeles Polytechnic. In my graduating class of 375 in June of 1942, there were only about twenty-five Japanese and thirty Negro students. To us Negroes the Japanese were "booches," or "Buddha heads." To them we were the "crocs," or "crocodiles." The names were used in fun, and no one grew angry over them. One time when we crocs and the booches were boasting of our achievements, a White student who used to hang around with us said: "Well, I'm just a poor peckerwood!" That broke us all up. In spring of 1942, just after Pearl Harbor, all of our Japanese friends were shipped off to Santa Anita Race Track and then to a relocation camp. Their pictures appeared in our 1942 high school yearbook, but they were nowhere to be seen on campus.

After assuring that Company L had sufficient trucks and the proper directions to get to Asciano, Executive Officer Major Sturdevant and Operations Sergeant Davis set out to find

Company K and Company I and get them to their objective as soon as possible. They found the two companies near Calci, about eight kilometers from Cascina, digging in for the night. Despite some of the men having been without sleep for thirty hours or more, there was no time for rest. Company K climbed onto the tanks and led off, with Company I following on foot. The column headed along the complicated route to Asciano under a moon-brightened sky.

Operations Sergeant Davis had the primary task of locating enemy and friendly positions for mapping purposes. He had help in determining the enemy position from Lieutenant Harrington, the intelligence officer. Davis, in my opinion, was the brains of the whole battalion. He put everything down in map form. He maintained our journal and all maps with great diligence and precision; when they would ask him to give a position, he would make a map showing it precisely. He always knew where our troops were and where the Germans were. He was so outstanding that he was one of very few given a Legion of Merit medal after we had been in combat for only two or three months. Davis was physically a very small man, in his early thirties. In my opinion, Colonel Daugette could not do anything without Sergeant Davis telling him what the layout was.

Colonel Daugette had another asset in Corporal James Motley, his jeep driver and orderly. Motley was a man of average size but very muscular. Like the colonel, he came from Alabama and was soft-spoken. Colonel Daugette had the largest bedroll I had ever seen; it looked larger than Motley when he carried it to and from the colonel's jeep each time we changed headquarters. The colonel always slept in a separate tent or room, and Motley cared for all of his personal needs. Two other jeep drivers were Adrian Dillon and James Rudd. Dillon drove Captain Shires's jeep, and Rudd was assigned to Lieutenant Harrington. Both men were able to maneuver their jeeps in and out of any situation.

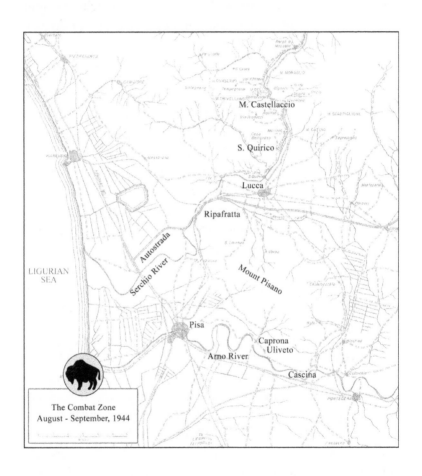

M. Castellaccio

S. Quirico

Lucca

Ripafratta

LIGURIAN
SEA

Autostrada

Serchio River

Mount Pisano

Pisa

Caprona
Uliveto

Arno River

Cascina

The Combat Zone
August - September, 1944

SEPTEMBER

By the evening of September 2, our infantry troops, along with tanks and engineers, had succeeded in taking Mount Pisano. In their withdrawal the Germans had left hundreds of mines and dozens of fields of barbed wire in strategic locations to impede our progress. They had blown every bridge across the Arno except for the Ponte Vecchio in Florence. The Ponte Vecchio was believed to have been built of wood by the Romans, destroyed later, and rebuilt in stone during the fourteenth century.

Because ours was the first unit of the Allies to cross the historic Arno River, Headquarters decreed that the Combat Infantryman's Badge—for exemplary conduct in action against the enemy—was to be awarded to each of the men who had made the initial crossing. The first five men to receive the badge were recognized on August 27. Recipients received an additional $10 per month.

As the 3rd Battalion began its offensive, we moved through the villages and towns of Lugnano, Uliveto, Caprona, and Asciano, all on the north side of the river east of Pisa. All along the way, hundreds of starving and cheering Italians surrounded our vehicles. They threw flowers at us and shouted, "*Viva Americani!*" They had been living behind German lines for months without adequate food. Even though they were allies of the Germans, they did not like the "Tedeschi," the Italian word for Germans.

Except for a few fascists, most of the people we encountered were truly happy to see us: they were free. Celebrations in each community seemed to grow as the morning progressed. At a hamlet just north of the Arno, the citizens greeted us with more cries of "*Viva Americani!*" "*Buon giorno!*" and phrases that were beyond our limited vocabulary. Others just waved happily. Some of the women could be seen crying. The excited civilians clung to our vehicles and showered the soldiers with grapes, flowers, and fruit. Some ran along, pouring wine for all who would accept it, while others of both sexes and all ages paid their tribute with hearty kisses. They had every guy in the column feeling like a conquering hero. Even today I smile and feel good when I recall those scenes. Here were White Italians greeting Negro Americans as liberators and showering us with love, while in our own country we remained second-class in all respects.

The vehicle I was riding in was fired upon by German 88s as soon as it left Lugnano, where I had given a starving priest a can of food. I remember that priest even today. He was thin, and his eyes and cheeks were sunken. He seemed embarrassed to be asking for a handout. We could hear the explosion of the 88s first and then the hiss of the incoming shell. All but one of us, Private Hiram MacBeth, a slow-moving, slow-talking Southern farm boy, got out of the truck and went to a prone position on the street. MacBeth remained in the truck, sound asleep. We joined him after a few rounds and continued quickly toward battalion headquarters. MacBeth remained asleep throughout the bombardment. That shelling was the first time I realized that the Germans were firing directly at me. Our vehicle passed through Pisa on its way to battalion headquarters. There, outside the walls of the Tower complex, I spoke with a Japanese-American soldier from the 100th Battalion. We crouched low to avoid being spotted and shot by snipers.

When we reached Asciano, the streets were so full of people that the troops could barely get through to the outskirts of town, where roadblocks had been set up. After a radio conversation with headquarters and a hurried consultation in the basement of the home of the local partisan leader, Major Sturdevant, Captain Reedy of Company K, and a tank commander assembled the troops again and continued toward San Giuliano, three kilometers to the northwest, with the mission of establishing a defense around the town.

By 0645, now-Captain Jarman had set up defenses around the north and west edges of San Giuliano. He and his men were joined by Captain Brown's Company L, which had come up on trucks. Our mission was suddenly changed: it was decided that we would attack rather than defend, and Companies I and L moved out with light and medium tanks at the head of each company. Company K under Captain Reedy was held in reserve.

Three casualties resulted from the first few rounds of enemy artillery before the infantry could deploy. Our advance developed into a dogged, house-to-house, barrier-to-barrier fight, with the enemy covering every avenue of approach with vicious crossfire and accurate mortar artillery barrages. One of the chief targets of the enemy artillery was the battalion outpost manned by the intelligence section, and when the M company commander, Captain Miles, left his jeep near the section headquarters, it was demolished by a direct hit.

In spite of the opposition, our advance was steady and, by 1600 hours, Brown and Jarman had moved forward three kilometers from San Giuliano and were digging in outside of Rigoli east of the Serchio River. The battalion had advanced fifteen kilometers from Cascina at the cost of one dead, twenty wounded, and one jeep destroyed. That night the front was comparatively quiet, although patrols could not advance because of enemy machine-gun fire. Jerry made our only supply route a dangerous road to travel by covering it with heavy artillery.

The next morning, September 4, at 1100, Colonel Daugette gave the order to continue the attack. Company K would advance on the left of the road, Highway 12, supported by tanks, and take the town of Ripafratta, just a few kilometers southwest of Lucca, while Company I on the right attacked a mountain mass designated as Hill 454. Two squads of A&P Platoon were attached to Company K, and one heavy machine-gun platoon of Company M was attached to each attacking company. Company L, which had borne the brunt of the previous day's attack, would remain in reserve.

The attack jumped off at 1210 hours, and Company K advanced steadily toward Molina di Quosa; then the advance slowed up, waiting for tank support that had been delayed because of mines near Rigoli and blown buildings further along the road. After careful reconnaissance, Company K continued without tanks, and by 2300 had secured Ripafratta. Major Aubrey R. Biggs, regimental executive officer, was killed at Ripafratta during heavy artillery bombardment, the first White officer to die in action, personally supporting I Company as tanks from the 1st Armored Division were assaulting the town. Biggs's body was brought to the aid station near battalion headquarters. I was at the station and saw that shrapnel in the head was the cause of his death. Lieutenant Colonel John Phelan replaced Major Biggs as the regiment's executive officer. Phelan was a large man in his thirties with a very athletic build. He was a West Point graduate, and we heard that he had been a heavyweight boxing champion at the academy.

The Germans were shelling our positions heavily. Private Robert Gilreath, a college boy who had come to I Company through the ASTP, was mortally wounded and died before he could be evacuated. Mac Scott told me he had been with Gilreath when Gilreath was hit. Mac and others had told Gilreath to hold on, but he died in their arms. Mac was to meet with a similar fate.

It was during the assault on Ripafratta on September 4 that we learned that the noise and dust generated by our tanks were the cause of the heavy German fire. Infantrymen learned to stay away from our advancing tanks. As soon as our tanks appeared, we knew that we had to get some shelter because the Germans were going to start firing at the tanks. They could hear them from a considerable distance or probably see their dust. All kinds of artillery would come flying in if a tank was anywhere near us. This created a dilemma for those troops attacking with tanks since tanks and infantry attacked as a team. The death of Major Biggs was a consequence of this kind of teamwork. Also, during the battle for Ripafratta, Jumbo Joe Fry, 1st Sergeant of Company K, showed outstanding leadership and later received a battlefield commission. Fry was from Pennsylvania.

Our entire battalion felt the weight of enemy artillery fire that day. We took more than five hundred rounds. I don't think there was an hour that passed from the time we went on line in August until the war ended when there was not artillery fire coming in or going out. We could always hear the artillery passing overhead and the hissing of the incoming shell. Then, of course, there was the explosion, and sometimes when it was close we could feel the debris from it. Mortars were different: you never knew where they were coming from. They would just start exploding around you. My father had been an officer in the 92nd Division artillery in France during World War I. He had told me that artillery fire overhead sounded like a freight train. He was right.

Company I had been having a difficult time advancing through the mountains east of Highway 12. The nature of the terrain and the distance made radio communication impossible and caused the men to lose contact with Company K. At 2300, Lieutenant Vernon Skinner of Company L led his platoon into the mountains to make contact with Company I and take them rations for the night.

Progress had been made on both flanks: on the left, the 100th Battalion had reached the bend in the Serchio River, near Monte San Quirico, where it leaves its southern course and sweeps west toward the sea; and the 81st Reconnaissance Battalion and the engineers had opened Highway 12 from San Giuliano halfway to the medieval city of Lucca, with its intact city walls thirty feet high, on the south bank of the Serchio River. (The city had once been ruled by a sister of Napoleon.) Second Battalion 370 was operating to the right of the highway, and we were making contact with them at Santa Maria.

On September 4 the Battalion command post moved to Villa Rossa on a hill above Rigoli, and Regiment ordered that we capture the fifteenth-century Villa Orsini and the village of Cerasomma, just east of the Serchio River north of Ripafratta. Reedy's Company K would continue on the left, and Jarman's I on the right, with Brown's Company L furnishing flank and rear protection. Our troops were now from one to four kilometers beyond the 100th Battalion on our left. Company K moved out by about 1400 hours, dogged by the heavy artillery fire that was tearing Ripafratta apart.

By 2000 hours, Company I was on to its objective, but Company K was forced to await nightfall before moving into Villa Orsini because of the deadly artillery barrages. Colonel Daugette and Captain Roane were pinned down for six hours during which Jerry threw everything from 20 mm to 210 mm shells. Not only Ripafratta but the entire battalion sector felt the weight of this onslaught.

At one time during the day it was planned to continue the attack on to Lucca, but the mission was canceled in favor of strong patrols in the direction of that city to determine enemy movements and strength. Outside of flank contact patrols, little could be done until Companies I and K had become set in their positions and supplied with rations, ammunitions, and the replacements that had just come forward.

Replacements were becoming necessary with the continued loss of men as the result of heavy shelling. Most of the replacements were men who had been overseas for a good while, but none had ever been in combat and few had received the necessary combat training. Their education began as soon as they ran the gauntlet of Ripafratta with the ration detail.

The next day, September 5, patrols were sent out in the direction of Lucca. The men returned with reports of enemy movement, small arms, and artillery fire up and down the road. There were also enemy observers in Nozzano, a town on the west side of the Serchio. We could see them sitting in bold arrogance in the tallest buildings, ready to call for artillery fire at our slightest movement.

A patrol from Company L found a steep bank of the river that served as a formidable barrier to attack in that direction. Our artillery was not in position to fire a counterbattery or knock out the outpost at Nozzano, and our tanks drew thundering artillery barrages everywhere they moved. With these factors in mind, Colonel Daugette decided to move the majority of the troops out of the bottleneck along the river onto the high ground to the east. From there, the river could be covered by fire, and the movement along the road would be cut to a minimum. The dampness and chilly nights would be uncomfortable; but this would be far preferable to the artillery making a rubble heap of Ripafratta and vicinity and filling the aid station with wounded and dying soldiers and civilians. By the end of the day, Lucca was in American hands, and the regimental command post was established in one of the city's hotels.

By dawn of September 7, all companies were in their new positions, and a party made up of Lieutenant Carter, transportation officer, and messengers from each company were guided by Operations Sergeant Davis through the mountains to establish a safer route of supply to the new locations. The necessity of carrying supplies over the rugged mountain trails, which were peopled by pitiful refugees, added another credential to the 3rd Battalion, which in effect became a mule train. It was something of a joke then, but that was before we had become fully aware of the cruel severity of the Italian mountains. We were rarely on level ground, and the Germans always chose the next higher hill or mountain so they could see and fire down on us.

The situation eventually began to look a little better. Tanks were getting hits on the enemy outposts, and we received word that our artillery would soon be in position to support us. Meanwhile the 434th Field Artillery Battalion, recently converted to infantry, had relieved the 100th Battalion and was patrolling our flank.

Early on the morning of September 10, the 3rd Battalion, less Company K, which was establishing a strong point at Villa Orsini, moved to the western gate of Lucca and reverted to regimental reserve. The move was without incident because the enemy had withdrawn. Our 370th Combat Team controlled Lucca. We immediately began tying together our loose ends, counting our losses, and reorganizing. The ten-day drive had cost us three dead and forty-nine wounded. One vehicle had been demolished and another damaged. Much equipment had been cached along the road during the advance and had to be retrieved. All our equipment needed cleaning. When we first entered combat, we all had gas masks. They were not heavy, but they were bulky; and we carried them over our shoulders in a canvas bag. We had all discarded them after we crossed the Arno. Reorganization was probably the most difficult job: selecting leaders to replace those who had fallen in battle and fitting the new men into their jobs so that each squad and platoon would form a smoothly working team. There had also been a change in the battalion staff. Major Sturdevant was transferred to the 2nd Battalion, leaving Captain Roane to serve as executive officer. Captain Pratt, who had been with the Regimental Operations Section, was sent to the battalion as S-3. These senior battalion officers were all White, and all had great respect for Staff Sergeant T. T. Davis, our operations sergeant.

Two days of resting, cleaning up, and making counterattack plans had quickly passed when orders from Regiment told us to move out the next morning in a new drive up the Serchio River Valley toward the Gothic Line. On September 13, visibility was still poor when Company I detrucked, six kilometers north of Lucca, formed a skirmish line, and moved on the hill mass that paralleled the Serchio. Part of the battalion staff had come with Company I, and Captain Roane established a command post in a large house on the side of a hill at San Alessio. Jerry almost immediately began to work over the area with heavy artillery. At regular three-minute intervals the shells roared in with the volume of a freight train, smashing over the command post and pounding the crossroads at San Michele. Later in the day, this command post was abandoned, and operations were carried on from a rambling old building near San Quirico, where First Sergeant Ross had established Headquarters Company. The battalion reserve company was also located in that vicinity. German resistance consisted of more than heavy artillery bombardment: we were aware of machine-gun emplacements in steel and concrete dugouts along with automatic weapons and mortars positioned to provide interlocking fire.

I was in the temporary command post in a very large villa when we were shelled 127 times (I counted), hits and near misses, by German artillery. Two very large rounds from German 11- or 15-inch railroad guns at Punta Bianca, a few miles to the northwest, fell on the soft ground in front of the house but did not explode. When the shelling stopped, I went outside and saw the cylindrical holes the shells had created. Had they exploded, everyone inside would have been killed. As it was, all of us in residence were covered with dust and debris from the crumbling structure. A German patrol began to encircle the villa, and we had to get out in a hurry. Captain Roane, battalion executive officer, picked me up in his jeep, knowing I had the battalion's maps. I had them because Operations Sergeant Davis had become ill and was sent back to the hospital. He had been on the job twenty-four hours a day since we entered combat and had become exhausted. I was given his job, and it was almost too much. I worked all night getting the maps ready to send to regimental headquarters. During that stretch, Captain Roane ordered the cooks, a surly group of soldiers reluctant to wait on a lowly corporal, to bring food to me while I worked.

On the road to a newly established command post, Captain Roane told the driver to take a left-hand turn. I told the captain that road headed north and would take us directly to the German lines. He ignored me. We continued for a few minutes until we were warned by the men in one of our outposts that we were approaching enemy lines. The captain was a nice guy and apologized for the mistake that could have cost our lives.

Sergeant Davis returned to duty after a few days, and no one could have been happier than I was.

Company I had been ordered to dig-in in the vicinity of Hill 105, a rocky knob overlooking the Serchio River that was dominated by Mount Castellaccio, 1,800 feet high, from which long-range machine-gun fire harassed our troops. Mount Castellacio was about six miles north of Lucca on the west bank of the Serchio River. (We gave certain of our objectives in the landscape names: hills were labeled Mexico, Canada, Georgia, Florida, Maine, and the like, and sometimes designated by numbers, such as 105, or by letters, such as Hill X or Y or Z.)

On the right flank, Company L advanced eight kilometers on September 14 to the high ground opposite Mount Castellaccio, taking moderate artillery fire. They overcame some enemy resistance in the vicinity of a large monastery and dug in for the night. The men were tired: only those who have fought all day over mountainous terrain can know just how tired one gets, but a change in plans made it suddenly necessary that Company L return to battalion reserve at Mt. San Quirico. It was a grueling march during which one man, Private Haywood Davis, was drowned while fording the Serchio River. (He is one of the 4,402 American GIs who lie in the American military cemetery south of Florence.)

Company K had taken up positions to the left of Company I; and still farther to the left, the 2nd Battalion of the 370th Infantry dug in. All were to keep on the alert against enemy infiltration and make every effort to determine enemy strength and disposition.

A strong patrol commanded by Lieutenant Christman, consisting of about two platoons of men from Companies I and M, attempted to reach the top of Mount Castellaccio but was driven back by machine-gun fire that wounded four. It was becoming more and more evident that this rocky objective was going to be tough to win.

During the early morning of September 16, Sergeant Henry Franklin and his comrades in I Company, from their position on Hill 105, saw a truckload of American soldiers drive into the town of Santa Maria Sesto, but they were too far away to render assistance when the truck was ambushed by the Germans. One man from the patrol, Fred Reaves, returned through Company I's position, and we learned that the ambushed party had been members of 2nd Battalion's Company F. A patrol from Company L went into the town to recover any wounded but saw no signs of friendly troops. Meanwhile, mortar and artillery fell with increased intensity from German positions on Hill 105. Henry Franklin was an ASTP soldier from Minneapolis. Like others who had been through the ASTP, he had advanced rapidly through the ranks since arriving in the division as a private in March.

It was clear that patrol activity was useless against the hill before us known as Mexico. It would take every weapon at our command to reduce the many machine guns, mortars, and light artillery pieces that the enemy had concentrated on the crest of this loaflike peak. Artillery did not seem to do any damage to the positions around the sinister thick-walled old castle atop the hill as burp guns and machine guns answered defiantly following each barrage from our 598th Artillery. Lieutenant Brown commanded the battalion's antitank platoon, but its guns failed to level the stone walls even with direct fire.

Regiment ordered a general attack by Company I, with machine guns and mortars from Company M to serve as a supporting force, while Company K and Company L pivoted to attack Mexico from the southwest. Second Battalion, on the left, would attack the hill behind Mexico that we had named Canada. Artillery and antitank guns would give direct support. Engineers were to accompany the attacking companies to neutralize mines and take care of demolition. Canada and Mexico were prominent hills on Mount Castellacio.

The time of the attack was set for 1000 hours on September 17. At 0910 the battalion command post was established at Villa Volpi, a vine-covered fifteenth-century house. Soon afterward Company K crossed the line of departure (LD) on time, and L followed as planned. As they advanced, Company I and Company M covered the objective with fire, receiving barrage after barrage in return. Within two hours Companies K and L were moving up the steep, terraced slope of Mount Castellaccio in the face of machine-gun and mortar fire. Two platoons of Company K were advancing on the southern end of the hill while another platoon was over on the western side. Company L was also on that side, receiving fire from the front and also from the hill on the left, which had not yet been assaulted by the 2nd Battalion.

By 1400 hours, elements of Company L were pressing the enemy so hard that Jerry was shelling the top of the hill even at the risk of his own troops. Company K could not advance because of wire and mines around the crest of the hill. Lieutenant Dempsey sent an urgent message calling for engineers. Meanwhile, several machine guns were sent to the aid of Company L, which had made its way close to the top of the hill but seemed unable to advance any further.

During the same attack, I escorted two soldiers from Company L to the battalion aid station. One of the men told me that he left the hill because it was getting dark and the Germans were counterattacking. The other soldier had shot off his thumb, bandaged it, and was seeking medical aid. It was hard to believe what individuals would do under severe life-threatening situations. After the war, when I became battalion sergeant major, I went around with our battalion adjutant to investigate what they called self-inflicted wounds. I discovered there were quite a few individuals who had wounded themselves, apparently to avoid combat.

When the attack seemed to have bogged down, orders were given to withdraw all troops to a safe distance so that more artillery could be placed on the objective. Meanwhile, companies were to organize for the renewal of the attack at 0530 the next morning. The night was marked by feverish activity to supply the frontline units with food and ammunition, to collect all of the wounded and dead, and to maintain adequate telephone and radio communication. Sergeant Joseph, the wire sergeant, and his wiremen worked unceasingly to restore wires that were constantly being cut by enemy shells, while Sergeant Otto Reed, radio repairman, labored by feeble candlelight to furnish the companies with short-range SCR 536 radios. Reed was also our company barber. While the battalion staff coordinated all of these functions, they still had to make plans for the morning attack. Company L's third platoon and a large part of the first platoon were still missing, but it was decided to go on with the attack as planned.

Promptly at 0530 on September 18, the attack began. Mortar and machine-gun fire were encountered, but the advance continued. At 0645 the advancing forces made contact with Captain Brown, who had located his third platoon. The platoon had spent the night in a covered position unaware of the withdrawal order. They were only three hundred yards southwest of the objective and were a welcome addition to the attacking force.

By 0900 hours a handful of brave men of Company L fought their way uphill to the castle. One of them, Sergeant Charles "Schoolboy" Patterson of Ft. Wayne, Indiana, rushed from cover, throwing hand grenades. He tossed a grenade into a machine-gun emplacement and then snatched a German machine gun from the site. Two other guns were destroyed, but fire was still coming from above the castle. Company K could not assist because they were pinned down by five machine guns hidden in deep emplacements on the crest of the hill. Patterson, who won a Silver Star for his gallantry, was an ASTP alumnus. After the war he moved to the San Francisco–Oakland area and became a successful businessman.

Battalion headquarters requested flamethrowers to use against enemy gun emplacements, but none were available in our sector. It looked as though we were stopped again, so orders were given to withdraw and reorganize. The first platoon of Company L had lost men but was still under control; the second platoon, which had stopped in a draw, contrary to the battalion CO's order, had been badly cut up by fire from the artillery and mortars located atop the hill. Company L's third platoon was out of contact. Company K was fairly well-organized but pretty badly shaken up.

As darkness came, more and more wounded were brought into the busy battalion aid station until nearly fifty men were accounted for in the two attacks on gun-studded Mexico. There were undoubtedly others; many men could not be accounted for.

Another attempt, our third, was made on Mexico at 0300 hours on the morning of September 19, but the tired troops were unable to get beyond the points previously reached. By 1000 hours, troops were again brought back, and our artillery gave Jerry a terrific pounding.

After almost one month in combat, a number of platoon leaders or lieutenants and platoon sergeants had been either wounded or killed. That had a demoralizing effect on the men. Sufficient replacements just weren't there, and those who arrived were truly green, with inadequate preparation. As I have noted, I had only eight weeks of infantry basic training myself. The fact is that the division was largely made up of guys who had scored low on the Army General Classification Test and the combat scene was more than they had ever expected. It is perhaps that reality that was, at least in part, responsible for subsequent charges leveled against the performance of the 92nd Division and about which more will be said in the pages ahead.

Word came from regimental headquarters that Major General Prichard, commander of the 1st Armored Division, was not in favor of any further attacks on the mountain, so plans were made to straighten our lines and allow the companies to get organized. Company L had reported nine more dead, and our battalion strength was lower than it had been since we came on line.

Company I was to continue to occupy Hill 105 and spread over to Hill 220, while Company K, on the left, took up positions to the west of Mexico on Mount Castellacio. M Company's heavy machine guns would be divided between the two companies. Company L would go into reserve at C. Vieri, a covered position near the forks in the road. Mortars and antitank guns would occupy favorable positions.

Company K moved into its new positions on the night of September 19, but Company L did not get itself together until the evening of the twentieth after a night-and-day search for Lieutenant Skinner and his 3rd Platoon, which had been in a house on the side of Mount Castellaccio for over two days without sufficient food and out of communication with the rest of the battalion. Five of Skinner's men were wounded, and it was a slow process getting everyone safely back to the rear through the intermittent shelling.

The new positions were hardly established when Colonel Daugette returned from regimental headquarters with the information that we were to take over the 2nd Battalion sector at once. From that time until September 25, we made one change after another. We were now responsible for nearly seven miles of a heavily wooded mountainous front that was in many places devoid of roads or well-defined trails. This front presented a tough supply problem for Lieutenant Oxley and his S-4 supply section. To keep from using Company L immediately, a hybrid company named X was organized, with Lieutenant Stokes of Company K commanding. Lieutenant Brooks, the battalion's A&P platoon leader, had the left platoon composed of the A&P, two BARs, two light machine guns from Company L, two heavy machine guns from Company H (2nd Battalion), and a squad from Company I. The overworked but well-organized 1st Platoon of Company L, under Lieutenant Horner, took the center position. They were strengthened by heavy machine guns from Company M. Lieutenant Butler, with the 1st Platoon of Company K and a section of heavy machine guns of Company H, formed the right platoon. Captain Reedy, K company commander, was to supervise this unit as well as G Company of the 2nd Battalion, now attached to the 3rd Battalion. As soon as the rest of Company L became organized, X Company was dissolved and its component parts went back to their proper units.

Despite the changing lines, patrols were going out regularly, making contact with the enemy and rounding up suspicious civilians for questioning by Lieutenant Harrington of 3rd Battalion's intelligence section. All reports indicated that the enemy was still in position, but there were indications of imminent withdrawal. In official circles, word came that Brigadier General John E. Wood, deputy commander of the 92nd Division, would take over command of this sector. General Almond visited the 3rd Battalion command post on September 25. We were still not part of the 92nd Infantry Division, although some of their top officers were in command.

On the night of September 25–26, it became evident that the Germans had begun a withdrawal; and before noon on September 26, Company I had verified that there was no enemy on Mount Castellaccio. Other patrols had also failed to make contact with Germans in their sectors.

A general advance was the order of the day. Before nightfall our men had made their way through mines and booby traps to the town of Val d'Ottavo and had reconnoitered the road along the Serchio River to find that large portions of it had been blown into the river, but it was in good shape north of our hill objective—Canada. If we could manage to get a jeep through to Val d'Ottavo, it would shorten our supply route and make it possible to use jeeps almost the entire distance. With this in mind, Captain Shires, with the help of the A&P Platoon, got three jeeps across the almost trackless hills. Even after we knew that Shires had achieved that, it still seemed impossible that a vehicle could climb those steep hills, squeeze through the narrow passages, and stick to the slippery clay banks.

Then, with the maddening perversity that sometimes characterizes military operations, Regiment called: "Third Battalion will be relieved by the FEB (The Brazilian Expeditionary Force). You are then to relieve the British Coldstream Guards on the 28th. An officer from Task Force 92 will furnish more details." That meant getting everything back down to a decent road with the utmost haste because the 28th was only a few hours away. Haste was hardly possible in the rain-filled darkness, and it was out of the question to move our jeeps all the way down before daylight. Company K could not do much moving around because of fire from an enemy SP (self-propelled) gun. We were somewhat relieved when Regimental Headquarters telephoned another order saying that we would go into an assembly area before going on line again.

The next day a company of Brazilians arrived, and after a linguistic tangle that involved everyone in the command post, we agreed—in English, Portuguese, Italian, and Spanish—that this company would relieve Company K. It seemed that the other Brazilian companies could not come because of the bad roads. Darkness and a rainstorm were fast approaching when Colonel Daugette, with a skeleton staff, led Company K and a few men from M and Headquarters Company across the Serchio River to an assembly area eight kilometers east of Lucca in the vicinity of Borgonuovo.

Relief by the Brazilians was almost comic. I was the only member of the battalion headquarters staff who spoke some Spanish and a little Italian. The Brazilian commander spoke a little Spanish, a little Italian, and Portuguese. The Brazilian commander and I talked and finally clarified our situation. I relayed this information to Colonel Daugette, and our relief by the Brazilians was completed. My high-school Spanish and one year of freshman Spanish at Berkeley had paid dividends!

At Borgonuovo we learned from Regimental command that one company from our battalion would entruck at 0500 on September 29 for a special mission up Highway 12 with the objective being Pievepelago, a mountain hamlet in the heart of the Northern Apennines. Two platoons of engineers were to accompany our men.

After finally rounding up the engineers and an ambulance, commanded by Lieutenant Cothren, Company K started on the trip to Prunetta, a village near Highway 12. Later Company I and part of Company M reported in with the information that the Serchio River was rising rapidly, making the ford all but impassable. It was decided to continue on with the troops we had and send Company L instructions from Sergeant Harris, intelligence sergeant, as to their next move after crossing the river.

Although Company L and the remnants of Battalion Headquarters Company were having difficulties after their relief by the Brazilians, they were also having fun. The river had become so swift that it was necessary to use winches to keep the loaded vehicles from being swept away. A Fox Movietone cameraman recorded the scene. Everyone was eager to get into the close-ups, hoping that some friend or relative back home would see him on the silver screen.

It was a long cold ride up Highway 12. Company K detrucked just south of Prunetta and continued on foot along the highway east of the Serchio. Progress was slow because of the many blown bridges and culverts and the danger of ambush. By 1700 the company was entering Mammiano Basso, where the men were met by artillery fire—the first opposition of the day. The artillery caused the company to become separated, and Sergeant Smith went back to bring the rear of the column forward. As he was entering the town with a group of stragglers, a friendly paisano signaled for them to stay close to the wall. Sergeant Smith ordered the others over, but before he could take cover a burp gun opened up, wounding his arm and side. The Jerries retreated when the fire was returned, leaving the town to Company K. During the firefight, Company I was sending a platoon ahead to make contact, and an hour later Company L arrived. A battalion command post was established at Prataccio, and plans for the next day were drawn up.

In the morning Company I occupied the town of Popiglio, and Company K continued to La Lima, discovering more blown bridges, mined roads, and evidence of hasty enemy withdrawal. Company L sent patrols to San Marcello Pistoiese but did not find the Germans who had been reported in that vicinity. Intelligence officer Harrington was close behind with a wire party, and he established a command post at Mammiano Alto that was later occupied for only a few moments when transportation moved in through the 1st Battalion sector on the right. It was a twenty-five-mile trip to get around six blown places in the main road. Several small villages and towns were on or near Highway 12, a key route through the Apennines just east of the Serchio River. We reached those places in pursuit of the Germans by army vehicle or on foot in areas where the bridges and road had been blown.

After passing Mammiamo Alto, there was no alternative but to follow winding route 12 as it hung precariously over Terme Lima, a rapid stream that roared out of the beautiful white-capped mountains that walled the valley. The retreating German engineers had a field day there, blowing up all bridges and causing landslides that blocked the road at regular intervals. Company L almost caught the retreating Germans at Cutigliano, when they blew the bridge practically in the face of Captain Brown's men, who had passed through Company K at La Lima. Company L then went to Ponte Sestaione and deployed along the road to Pian

Degli Ontani. Company I occupied Cutigliano while Company K went to Vizzaneta and sent patrols under Sergeant Collins and Sergeant Stripling high into the rugged mountains. No enemies were found, and all efforts were bent toward repairing the roads and bringing up supplies. Captain Pratt organized every available paisano and soldier and soon had the road open for jeeps, an important accomplishment as this was one of the Fifth Army's northernmost spearheads.

The 3rd Battalion had succeeded in breaching the famed German fortifications of the Gothic (sometimes called Green) Line. The men of the 3rd Battalion moved quickly and pressed the retreating Germans. We surprised them with our ability to move fast and maneuver our vehicles over impossible terrain. The Germans continued to demolish the road before us. Patrols to Piansinatico, Campetti, and Costa by Companies L and I revealed that the enemy was still to our front, determined to make a stand in the mountains, and it looked like we would be there quite a while. But it didn't work out that way. Newly arrived duffel bags, containing a change of uniform, underwear, and sundries, had been available to the men only one day when the 3rd Battalion was relieved by the 39th Anti-Aircraft Artillery Regiment, a British unit converted to infantry. We received orders from 92nd Division headquarters that we were to return to the coastal region north of the resort town of Viareggio. Our battalion was now about thirty miles from the coast, deep in the heart of the Apennines. We could not return directly because Highway 12, the usual route, was blocked by landslides, blown bridges, and other consequences of war. We had to take the long way around through Montecatini, a city east of Lucca along the Autostrada. It was nearly one hundred miles back to Viareggio via a winding, steep, treacherous ride in the numbing cold of the high mountains, then a fast run along the Autostrada north of Pisa to Lucca through the rain and darkness to our destination. As we approached Lucca we were able to see in the distance and through the mist the ancient Roman aqueducts, which were in ruins but still majestic. Our advance party, intended to help us to our destination, had stationed guides; but Viareggio, which was soon to become the headquarters of the 92nd Division, seemed the center of great confusion, and no one seemed to know anything of the general situation, much less where we were to go.

We finally learned that Captain Shires, S-1, and the battalion executive officer were in the vicinity of Pietrasanta, six miles north of Viareggio, and that there had been a last-minute change in regimental plans. It was 2200 hours before the battalion finally arrived in the area selected for bivouacking and much later by the time shelter could be found from the rain that threatened. We were all dead tired by then.

After just over five weeks of combat, Combat Team 370 had suffered 263 casualties: 19 dead, 225 wounded, and 19 missing. There were also a number of noncombat casualties, including the sick and those who were otherwise injured.

As a long jumper, University of California at Berkeley

My mother, Doris T. Houston, and I at our home 950 E. 42nd Place in Los Angeles. Behind us is our 1937 Plymouth, "The Gray Mist." June, 1944

My proud mother's photo-tapestry of her youngest soldier son

Men of the 92nd Division crossing the Arno, August 1944

This combat patrol advanced three miles north of Lucca to contact an enemy machine gun nest. Here, a bazooka-man cuts loose at the target some 300 yards distant. (U.S. National Archives)

German prisoner wearing civilian clothes sits in a jeep at south gate of walled city of Lucca, Italy, awaiting removal to a rear area.

Buffalo Soldier escorting German prisoners' of war.

Truman Gibson, civilian aide to Secretary of War Henry L. Stimson During World War II. (Project Gutenberg eBook of Integration of the Armed Forces, 1940-1965)

Cascina area, Italy. Two columns of Company I, 3rd Battalion, 370th Regiment, ford the Arno River unopposed, as the U.S. Fifth Army advances against the Germans, September 1, 1944. (U.S. National Archives)

Cascina area, Italy. Two columns of Company I, 3rd Battalion, 370th Regiment, ford the Arno River unopposed, as the U.S. Fifth Army advances against the Germans, September 1, 1944. (U.S. National Archives)

Wearing the sweater Grandma made for me, December 1944

Sketch by an Italian street artist, early 1945

Members of a mortar company of the 92nd Division pass the
ammunition and heave it over at the Germans in an almost
endless barrage near Massa, Italy. This company is credited with
liquidating several machine gun nests. (U.S. National Archives)

Author on leave in Rome, April 1945

"Genoa, Italy. In this newly liberated city, the 92nd Division troops enter the Galleria Guiseppe [sic] Garabaldi." (U.S. National Archives)

Lt. Col. Marcus Ray as a civilian. Ray commanded the 600th Field Artillery Battalion of the 92nd Infantry Division. (Project Gutenberg eBook of Integration of the Armed Forces 1940-1965)

Maj. Gen. Edward M. Almond at ceremony honoring 92nd Division Soldiers, Spring 1945 (U.S. National Archives)

The author (on left) with a fellow G.I. at the Tower of Pisa, 1945

Before a map of the areas in which our 3rd Battalion fought in Italy. Mosaic relief at the American Military Cemetery in Florence. (Photo by Philippa Houston, 1993)

Author at the Cinquale Canal, western edge of the Gothic Line.
(Photo by Ivan A. Houston, 2002)

The Serra River flows through Seravezza, Italy, at the point where I crossed with the ammunition detail in October 1944, Mount Cauala rises sharply on the right. This photo was taken in October 2002, fifty-eight years later. I remembered a wall like the one shown here on the river's edge. (Photo by Ivan A. Houston, 2002)

The American Military Cemetery at Florence, Italy, 2007

The grave of Capt. Jesse Jarman, 370th Infantry Regiment, 92nd Division (Photos by Dianne & Bud Schwarzbach, 2007)

John Mack of the Urban League, Rep. Juanita Millender-McDonald, and I with Vernon Baker, a former member of the 370th Infantry Regiment. Mr. Baker received the Congressional Medal of Honor from President Bill Clinton in 1997 for his gallantry in action near Viareggio, Italy in 1945.

Author's Father, 2nd Lt. Norman O. Houston, 92nd Division, Headquarters Detachment, 317th Ammunition Train, American Expeditionary Forces

Author at African American Civil War Monument, Washington, DC. Inset, engraved on monument, "Benjamin F. Talbot,", author's great grandfather, soldier in the 5th Colored Regiment. (Photo, 2009, Ivan A. Houston)

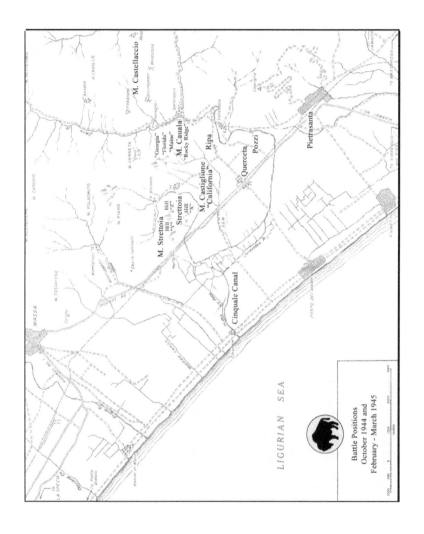

M. Castellaccio

M. Cauala
"Rocky Ridge"

"Georgia"
"Florida"
"Maine"

Ripa

M. Castiglione
"California"

Querceta

Pozzi

M. Strettoia

Hill
"Y"

Strettoia
Hill
"X"

Pietrasanta

Cinquale Canal

MASSA

LIGURIAN SEA

Battle Positions
October 1944 and
February - March 1945

OCTOBER:
MOUNT CAUALA,
SERAVEZZA,
AND "MELTING AWAY"

On October 3, Colonel Frank E. Barber, the 92nd Division's chief of staff, was killed. He was replaced by Lieutenant Colonel William J. McCaffrey, father of General Barry McCaffrey, who served as President Clinton's drug czar after retirement from the military. Major Thomas St. John Arnold, who had been executive officer of the 598th Field Artillery Battalion, was promoted to assistant chief of staff of the 92nd Infantry Division. Arnold, who later retired as a colonel, is the author of *Buffalo Soldiers: The 92nd Infantry Division and Reinforcements in World War II, 1942–1945*, c. 1990, Sunflower University Press, ISBN 0-89745-127-9. Colonel Arnold's book has been a great help in fleshing out division details from the journal maintained at 3rd Battalion headquarters.

On October 5, the 370th Infantry Regiment established its command post near Pietrasanta. It had fought its way north along Highway 12, deep in the Apennine mountains, interrupting a chief route of German communications. The 317th Combat Engineer Battalion and 598th Field Artillery Battalion had provided great support, the former by clearing minefields and building bridges and the latter by using its 105-mm howitzers with great efficiency and effect.

Also on October 5, the 370th Combat Team became a part of Task Force 92, under General Almond. Its mission was to control Mount Cauala, a mass of rugged terrain 1,200 feet high with a ledge two-thirds up that was soon labeled Rocky Ridge. Mount Cauala, three miles north of Pietrasanta, overlooked the flat coastal plain that ended at the Ligurian Sea. The mountain was perceived as the first objective on the way to capturing the city of Massa.

Task Force 92 included the 370th Regimental Combat Team, comprising the 598th Field Artillery Battalion; the 2nd Armored Group's 434th and 435th Anti-Aircraft Artillery Battalions, which were converted to infantry; the 751st Tank Battalion; the 894th Tank Destroyer Battalion; 179th Chemical Company; C Battery 351st Anti-Aircraft Artillery Battalion; C Battery 450th Anti-Aircraft Artillery Battalion; and 2nd Company 23rd Engineer Battalion (Italian). Together we formed a six-mile front with the coastal plain on our left and the Northern Apennines on our right.

On October 6, Task Force 92 initiated its attack on Mount Cauala, first of several mountains guarding the southern approach to Massa. It was believed that by taking Mount Cauala we could move north along Highway 1, take Massa, and move on to La Spezia. The 1st Battalion was in reserve south of Viareggio, the 2nd Battalion was in line north of Pietrasanta, and the 3rd Battalion was moving toward the coast from its previous position in the Serchio Valley. The 598th Field Artillery accompanied the 3rd Battalion. Opposing the American forces was Germany's 42nd Jaeger Division, comprised of Russian, Polish, and Alsatian prisoners of war conscripted into the German Army.

Ulysses Lee has written in great detail about these critical days and the performance of Negro troops in the 92nd Division's march north. Lee is the author of *The United States Army in World War II: Special Studies. The Employment of Negro Troops*, published by the Center of Military History, United States Army, Washington, D.C. Library of Congress Catalog Card Number: 66-60003 First Printed 1966-CMH Pub 11-4. Available from the Superintendent of Documents, U.S. Government Printing Office, Washington, DC 20402.

At the time of publication, Lee was professor of English at Morgan State College. He had served in the army during World War II, rising from lieutenant to major as an education officer and editorial analyst in the field and in the headquarters of Army Service Forces. For seven years after the war, he was the military history specialist on Negroes in the army.

It was on October 6, 1944, according to Lee (p. 547), that "Evidences of a growing malaise within the combat team began.... They continued to manifest themselves through the month as one after another of the combat team's units went up the slopes of Mount Cauala and neighboring heights and came down again for an infinite variety of reasons, only a few of them definitely connected with the increased tenacity of the enemy, who had decided to defend this end of the Gothic Line vigorously."

Page 549: "It was a problem in faith and the lack of it—the wavering faith of commanders in the ability and determination of subordinates and enlisted men, and the continuation in the minds of enlisted men of training period convictions that they could not trust their leaders. Disorganization born of desperation soon manifested itself throughout the task force." Lee goes on to cite acts of great bravery and heroism by Negro troops but concludes that low test scores and poor motivation were insufficient explanation of the troops' failure to perform. Rather, he says, the cause was "an all pervading lack of trust, beginning in the training period. . . .It was not long before neither the men nor the officers of the division were convinced that a given job would be done and, in some instances, that it was worth the trying."

Lee's analysis was news to me. He speaks of a large-scale loss of contact between officers and troops, general disorganization, and the failure of men to move forward when directed. I did observe problems of morale and evasion of responsibility that developed later and which I will comment on, but I saw no reluctance of men to move forward when ordered to do so.

First Lieutenant Alonzo M. Frazier, a Negro officer and one of the 1st Battalion's platoon leaders, was among the men who died on October 6 as Combat Team 370 began its attack on Mount Cauala. Frazier was mortally wounded but refused a medical corpsman's offer to take him to the rear. He lies in the American military cemetery at Florence. We had heard that the 1st Battalion had suffered heavy casualties trying to capture a mountain near the town of Seravezza. Our goal was to reach Seravezza and relieve and support the 1st Battalion in the attack on Mount Cauala.

October 7 was spent getting oriented and obtaining better living quarters for the troops. Company I was still under regimental control, working with a tank battalion, and it looked as if the remainder of the battalion would attack in the morning, but this plan was canceled. Meanwhile, we were quartered in the northwest end of Pietrasanta—a busy town filled with civilians and overflowing with infantry and tanks. Jerry knew this too and harassed the place daily with heavy artillery, causing a number of casualties. At the north end of Pietrasanta, near a town called Querceta, there was a factory housing huge slabs of Carrara marble that had been quarried from the mountains above. As I headed to the battalion outpost just north of Querceta, the Germans began shelling. I ducked into the factory as the shelling continued. When the slabs of marble began getting hit, the shards of stone struck like shrapnel and the shelling became even more dangerous. I got out of there in a hurry.

In Pietrasanta we relieved a British unit during a period of heavy shelling by the Germans. It was afternoon and, despite the bombardment, the British paused for tea. I was invited to join them as the area around us seemed to explode, yet none of us was hurt or even excited during that curious and even surreal respite.

Also during our stay in Pietrasanta, First Sergeant Edward Ross and I were standing next to a wall outside our battalion command post. An artillery shell landed on the other side of the wall, and the explosion lifted us into the air and settled us gently onto the ground. The air was sucked out of our lungs. We both checked our limbs to see if all was well and then went back to work as if nothing had happened. Some members of our headquarters team were wounded in the explosion. Sergeant Ross was slightly wounded later during our time in Italy and became quite angry when he learned that the War Department had notified his mother and thus upset her. Sergeant Ross was always neat and cleanly shaven, with a mustache that was trim even in combat.

The next day, all except Company I engaged in personal care, cleaning of equipment, and reorganization while the staff made a reconnaissance of the front lines north of Pozzi, where 2nd Battalion had taken positions. The proposed attack still did not develop, and the night passed without incident.

Our idleness ended when Colonel Sherman suddenly called for a company to meet him on the mountain above Capezzano, one mile east. Company I kept the rendezvous and was sent off up the mountain trail. The rest of the battalion was ordered to follow them and by dusk had caught up with the tail end of

Company I. Shortly after darkness, it became apparent that they were having trouble up ahead, and we learned that there was no longer a guide with Company I but that they were relying on the meager directions given them before starting. The trail we were following seemed the wrong way to Seravezza, our destination, and because it was too dangerous to do any exploring in the pitch-black darkness we were ordered to bivouac for the night and set out again at dawn.

The next morning we picked up the trail and after four hours of rough going reached L'Argentiera, a rural community that we decided to use as a base for operations in Seravezza. The troops got some much-needed rest during the day, and at 1900 hours the battalion moved out for Seravezza with the plan to join 2nd Battalion there and attack Mount Cauala near midnight on October 11, 1944.

I was with the battalion's intelligence squad as we made our way toward Seravezza, at the base of Mount Cauala on its eastern side, at the confluence of the Sera and Vezza rivers. Though Seravezza was only three miles from Pietrasanta, the road between the two towns was under consistent enemy fire and we had to use a narrow, winding mountain trail that would have been too much even for mules. We were still on our way when darkness descended. It was raining in torrents, and absolutely nothing was visible. It took four hours to go three kilometers, and then we found that only half of the battalion was present. By the time everyone had been rounded up, the Sera River had risen to where it could no longer be forded, and it was necessary to call off the attack until the next night. After an hour of feeling ahead for each step, we had lost all sense of proportion, and drops of two or three feet in the torn-up road seemed like chasms. The sound of the Vezza River on our left was a menacing roar. Men stumbled, fell, and lost equipment that could not be found in the mud and darkness. Flashes of lightning only served to blind and confuse the senses with their brilliance. I followed a scout named

Sweeney, who was a good friend but careless. He lost contact with the man in front of him, and all of us behind him were lost in the dark in the fierce rainstorm. Completely soaked, about a dozen of us stumbled around until we found an abandoned shack near the Sera River and rested until daybreak before moving on to find our command post in Seravezza. Headquarters had not foreseen the blackness of that awful night. The thunder sounded like artillery fire, and the lightning lit up the mountains above the town.

When we entered Seravezza, we were surprised to encounter our regimental commander, Colonel Sherman. He had come over the trail with part of our battalion, and he cautioned us to avoid exposure since all of Seravezza was under observation by the Germans, who were sweeping the streets with machine-gun fire and had already wounded some of our men. I may owe my life to Colonel Sherman; after that I wondered often what he was doing up there with the rest of us. We found our battalion's headquarters in an abandoned school.

Mount Cauala dominated Seravezza, and every move that our troops made in the shattered town was visible to the enemy in the hills above. Medium and heavy artillery raked the buildings at regular intervals, and small-arms fire swept the streets if men exposed themselves. Careful reconnaissance was made for observation posts (OPs) and approaches to the river crossing, and company commanders were given the plan of attack. Company I would attack Mount Cauala on the right, L in the center, and K on the left. K Company would lead out, carrying the telephone wire for communication.

It was 2310 hours before the last man had slipped into the icy waters of the Sera River and climbed the specially constructed ladders necessary to negotiate the steep, rough climb up the mountain. It was as steep as Mexico had been on Mount Castellacio, and knife-edged rocks ripped clothing and tore flesh as the men tried to get a footing in the blackness. Great difficulty was experienced in keeping platoons and squads together, and once-separated leaders did not know whether their men had turned back, been hit by the enemy machine-gun fire that spattered the trails, or had missed their footing and plunged to the rocks below. Calls to each other only drew more accurate enemy fire. By 0455 hours Company K was on top of Mount Cauala, and the other two companies were still climbing but losing men regularly. Lieutenant Christman returned to the line of departure to locate a platoon of men who had been caught in machine-gun fire. He knew that at least four had been wounded. Companies I, K, and L were all atop the mountain by 0730 hours on October 12.

With the coming of daybreak, the Germans had begun to counterattack on the mountain. Bill Rich, a corporal I knew in K Company, told me when he came off the hill later that morning that the Germans had kept coming despite our heavy fire. He thought they were fanatics. One group came from the south and attacked Company K, while others appeared on the knob above Company I. Company M engaged them with mortar fire while Company F, 2nd Battalion, started up the mountain to assist Company I since only about one squad was there to hold the enemy. Request was made that 1st Battalion send a force from the south to encircle the Germans at that point. The help from the 1st Battalion did not come, and it remained for a few valiant men from Companies L and K to repulse the repeated counterattacks from three different directions. German mortar fire and grenades could not dislodge our men, and they stuck to their position throughout the afternoon despite dwindling ammunition supplies. Private Jake McInnis of Company K was one of the mainstays in this defense, personally killing over a dozen Germans with his BAR before being knocked out by a concussion grenade. He was taken to the rear but returned days later. His stand that day earned him a Silver Star.

Those in command in Seravezza, at the foot of the mountain where counterattacks were taking place, were being lashed by terrific artillery fire but were unaware of the plight of the men on the hill. They dispatched Private Hopkins of Company L and Private Mosby of Company K with messages requesting guides for ration parties that night. The messengers found Jerry emplacements between them and their companies and could not get through. An ammunition detail made up of every available individual, including yours truly, had been forced off the hill, with one killed and several wounded by enemy fire.

I had volunteered for the ammunition supply detail with about a dozen men. I carried a metal box of ammunition in each hand. The boxes were rectangular and weighed about twenty-five pounds each. I loosened the sling on my M-1 rifle and slung it over my back. The first time I saw the Germans up close and shooting at us was at Seravezza. As we approached the hill, we looked up and could see a German machine gun raking our position. There were two German soldiers manning the gun, and our fire hit one. The other carried him away, and we continued toward our goal. When we reached the base of the hill, the Germans unleashed a tremendous artillery barrage. We crouched for a time and then continued on our way. Halfway up the hill we encountered more machine-gun fire and mortars. Shrapnel was flying all around and some of it, quite hot, landed on my clothes, burning through to the skin. Some in our detail were hit. The detail could not continue and returned to the base of the hill. We had failed in our mission to supply ammunition, and soon other men from the rifle companies were coming off the hill. It became a mess. I will never forget the smell of burning gunpowder as the shells exploded all around us. I lost my appetite for several weeks after this experience. For a while I thought I had been gassed; however, it was the burning cordite that came from the exploding shells that had made me ill.

At about 1600 hours, a heavy barrage of our own artillery fell short and struck the entrenched remnants of our Companies K and L. That was more than the tired men could take, and they withdrew at the first opportunity. Another counterattack developed soon after. It looked for a moment that the Germans would advance clear into Seravezza as our withdrawing troops came off the hill. The battalion staff hastily organized them into platoons and put them in defensive positions in various parts of the town. Even the battalion command post became a strong point.

Darkness fell, and the counterattack did not develop. Every effort was made to get all of our known wounded in from the battlefield—nobody knew how many had been casualties—and round up the victims of shock, who were moving aimlessly about with the horror of battle in their eyes. We had an excellent medical officer in the 3rd Battalion—Captain Young. He served with us throughout combat. He had a contingent who handled all of the wounded, and sometimes they would bring in someone who was dead but not yet recognized as such. Captain Young was stationed not too far from battalion headquarters.

Captain Miles of Company M stuck to the often-shelled river crossing for hours, directing the rescue of wounded and reassuring the dazed men as they came down the hill. Captain Jarman of Company I had only fourteen men with him when he returned with the news that Captain Gandy, a first battalion company commander, had received a mortal wound while leading his company up the hill. I had seen Gandy moving up when I was with the ammunition detail. He was apparently wounded just moments later. Machine-gun fire in that sector had cut up the two companies from many different directions, keeping them pinned down the entire day. For a time we thought at battalion headquarters that Captain Reedy of K Company was on the hill with his men, but then we learned that he had been seen at the bottom of the hill being helped across the stream by one of his enlisted men. Earlier, Major Sturdevant was heard saying, "Men coming off the hill should be hit on their head with a rifle butt."

Despite several efforts, we were never able to take and control Mount Cauala. The Germans repelled every daylight attack, and in the end they controlled the mountain.

Our battalion never quite recovered from the battle at Seravezza. We lost many men and officers, and there were no infantry-trained replacements. Combat Team 370 was in poor condition. The 1st and 2nd battalions also lost a number of outstanding leaders. Ulysses Lee has written (p. 552), "Enlisted replacements were few and those who did arrive seldom provided better material. Many of those arriving were AWOLs from the East Coast Processing Center and rehabilitees from the African Disciplinary Barracks. Most of them, unhappy to find themselves in a front-line regiment, 'growled a great deal.' It became easier for the older members of the combat team to listen to their gripes." I never knew the source of our replacements, but I am certain they could not have received the quality of training that we received at Fort Huachuca.

Regiment ordered the 3rd Battalion to assemble again at L'Argentiera, a rural community. As each company accounted for as many men as possible, it was sent back. By 0710 the battalion had closed in on the supply base where Sergeant Jackson, battalion supply sergeant, and Sergeant Blake, the antitank platoon sergeant, had been collecting food and ammunition. Two platoons transported it over the mountain from Pietrasanta by mule train.

Other than a few small patrols and some security posts set up by Company M, there were no operations for the day and most men could enjoy the remarkable peace of L'Argentiera and prepare for the tough march back over the mountains to Pietrasanta. A farmer had rigged up a lightbulb to a generator that was run by a waterwheel. The bulb was in a shed, and all of us stood in awe as the bulb gave off a white light. We had become so used to candles that the brilliant light from electricity seemed like a miracle and something we had never seen before. The Italian mountains concealed this very peaceful meadow just a few miles from the fierce fighting in Seravezza. The scene was surreal.

We started up the long trail just before dark, and it was 0300 hours the next day before the battalion closed in on Pietrasanta to end one of the most grueling and costly engagements that we had experienced since entering combat. The Seravezza casualty report showed the following:

	WOUNDED		MISSING		DEAD	
	Enlisted Men	Officers	EM	OFF	EM	OFF
Company I	15	1	4	1	0	0
Company K	17	2	7	0	1	0
Company L	10	2	10	0	1	1
Company M	3	0	2	0	0	0

Most of those listed as missing were later confirmed as killed in action. Lieutenant Lionel Ladmirault of Company I, a Louisiana Negro with blue eyes, blond hair, and white skin; Lieutenant Ralph Skinner of Company L; and Pfc. Hugh Portee were also killed in action. Lieutenant Skinner, although mortally wounded, continued to lead his men against a German counterattack until he died. He was awarded the Silver Star posthumously. Private first class Portee was near me during our effort to supply ammunition at Seravezza. I knew he had been hit during a period of heavy fire, but I was unaware until later that he had died. The battalion suffered seventy casualties in just one day, and there were scores of men suffering from battle shock and fatigue. I was probably in shock but did not know it. Numbers alone can never tell the cost in suffering, broken spirit, and the loss of experienced soldiers.

The battle at Seravezza delivered a crushing blow to the 3rd Battalion. There was anger among the troops because we felt we were being sent into impossible situations—suicide attacks. We knew that the Germans knew where we were and that we were going to be heavily bombarded, and we did not have sufficient firepower or manpower to respond. In brief, we were outgunned. Our morale clearly dropped after Seravezza. For four days the 3rd Battalion reorganized, reequipped, trained, took showers, and caught up on lost sleep. It was our first real break after fifty days of combat, but we were still harassed almost daily by artillery fire.

During this time I was in battalion headquarters recording information we were receiving from runners and by phone and walkie-talkie. Sometimes I accompanied Captain Shires to the front line. In one instance a report came in that one of our men was killed from the blast of a bazooka. Shires and I went to check that out. We found a dead soldier who had been covered and placed on a litter. We got his dog tags, and I helped carry him to a vehicle that took him to the rear. Captain Shires talked to the officer in charge in an effort to find out how the accident had happened. We learned that the GI was just standing in the wrong place when the bazooka was fired. Bazookas—portable rocket launchers—were introduced to us after we entered combat. They were designed to help infantrymen fight tanks.

On October 17, the regimental commanding officer reported that General Almond would inspect the battalion at 1300 hours. The inspection would include ordnance, vehicles, and so forth. The men were to be prepared for another attempt to take Mount Cauala. Motor Officer Lt .Charles "Cutes" Carter was to be in the rear area with the vehicles for their inspection. We were required to look neat and our equipment, namely guns, had to be clean during an inspection. The inspecting officer could snatch the weapon from any soldier, hold it up, and look down the barrel to see if it was clean. The general's aide was with him to take notes.

General Almond appeared promptly and marched up and down our formations. Colonel Daugette and each company commander accompanied him. The general stopped in front of me and asked how long I had been with the battalion. He talked to my commanding officer, Captain Shires, and with Colonel Daugette, and ordered them to award me the Combat Infantryman's Badge "for exemplary conduct in action." I guess the award was for trying to get ammunition onto the hill above Seravezza and for surviving almost two months of continuous combat. At any rate I did receive the much-sought-after badge and $10 more in pay each month. After the war all who had received the Combat Infantryman's Badge were entitled to a Bronze Star upon request. I received my Bronze Star medal, years later, from the War Department.

Late on October 17 our battalion began the relief of the 1st Battalion and occupied the positions that they had been holding on Mount Cauala for about six days. The 1st Battalion's command post was at Pozzi. The enemy's emplacements were generally on an east-west line starting at the base of the hill labeled Maine on the right, stretching to a small loaflike hill on Mount Castiglione called California in the center, and on to Alaska, a sprawling three-peaked mass that spread in a northwesterly direction until it touched Highway 1. Nestled in the valley between Maine and Alaska, but almost as high as California, was the town of Strettoia. To the south the country was flat farmland and olive groves, crisscrossed by sunken roads and canals and dotted by a few houses and three communities. Querceta, the largest, was on Highway 1. A good road led from there to Ripa, then only a heap of rubble; and from Ripa a winding road led to Pozzi, one kilometer south. All of this territory was under enemy observation. The train station in Querceta had been blasted into rubble. The steel tracks were twisted. The trees in the area had been shredded by shrapnel.

Company I went into the right sector with its right flank on the Seravezza River; K took the center just south of California;

and L took the left over to Highway 1 and made contact with the 434th AA Regiment on our left. Company M's first and second platoons went to K and L sectors, and the mortars of Company M took up positions from which they could support the entire front. The battalion command post, Headquarters Company, the medical aid station located at Pozzi, along with the headquarters of the 751st Tank Battalion and the 1st Platoon of the 894th Tank Destroyer Battalion, were all under the direction of a Major Fine. I never met him.

As soon as the 1st Battalion was relieved, we sent squad patrols out from each company to feel out the enemy and take advantage of any opportunity to better our position. Company I managed to get a platoon on the "Brown Spot" on Maine (an area of no vegetation) and Company K occupied California without difficulty, so Company L was ordered to occupy Fosso Bonazzera north of Pozzi in order to straighten out the lines. Later, Company I was able to occupy parts of the western slope of Mount Cauala and make contact with Company K.

On October 17, Company K was ordered to showers. The Battalion CO and S-3 went to Pozzi to check on details of the relief. They obtained map overlays from Operations Sergeant Davis and the intelligence sergeant.

October 18 found us at Pozzi. By 1100, Company K's reconnaissance patrol reported enemy emplacements, barbed wire entanglements, and a few mines, but no sign of the enemy. Without mortars, Company K occupied enemy positions. Heavy machine guns from Company M were not yet in position. Shortly after 1600, shells began landing two or three hundred yards forward of the command post. They were from a high-velocity weapon. Captain Jarman sent out his 3rd Platoon to occupy the position on Mount Cauala designated Rocky Ridge, the point being shelled by the Germans.

Just before 7:00 AM on October 19, Company K brought in four prisoners who had surrendered, claiming that they had been sleeping in holes and without much food. They had come from Maine on Mount Cauala. Moments later, Company L brought in three more Germans who had walked into L's command post waving a white flag. An additional eight prisoners said they had been among a group of thirteen; the eight said they had spent the entire night waiting to surrender because of the artillery fire. We had no idea what had happened to the other five.

After almost two months in line, those of us in battalion headquarters were sent to the showers. We were dirty and desperately needed a change of clothing. Shower companies staffed by Negro soldiers were set up in a rear area. We showered with hot water, which was unavailable at the front, and real soap. We received a change of underwear and clean combat uniforms. This did wonders for morale. The showers and the distribution of clean clothes took place in tents and trailers set up by the service corps. The whole procedure did not take long. The troops handling both the showers and the distribution of clothing seemed very efficient.

We continued our patrolling and shelling activities against Mount Cauala and shelled Maine with tremendous force. Company K's patrol on October 19 returned without having encountered any of the enemy, while a patrol of Company L located mines and booby traps along with wire too heavy to cut. Artillery and Bangalores were used to detonate the barbed wire. Bangalore torpedoes were lengths of pipe screwed together. They were filled with charges, shoved under barbed wire, and detonated.

Captain Jesse Jarman received the Bronze Star on October 20 for his heroic achievements in action. He was a slight, youthful, light-skinned Negro officer whose captain's bars shone like the sun. Lieutenant Isaac Jones of I Company, who had been in the hospital, returned to duty. Jones was a very affable and mild-mannered officer who had been adopted as a waif by a mathematics professor at Howard University in Washington, D.C. Both Jarman and Jones, the cream of the crop, would be killed in action months later as we struggled in the Apennine Mountains.

Beginning at 2100 hours on the night of October 21, Company L, under Captain Clarence Brown, accompanied by a platoon of engineers, was blowing an area of dense barbed wire and moving along through minefields toward its objective on Mount Strettoia, adjacent to Mount Cauala. A platoon of Company L, under Lieutenant Reuben L. Horner, made it through the now-open area and fought off eight enemy counterattacks on Mount Strettoia while awaiting support from another unit that failed to locate it. This platoon remained in place until it had used all its ammunition. Horner sent this handwritten message:

Colonel Daugette: Am sending the prisoners and wounded before dawn. I have not received ammunition nor grenades. With each counterattack, more and more of my men slip off the hill to safety. I can't hold the area that I have with so few men and with dark more men will slip off. I've done all I could with the men and ammo and I'll stay as long as I can. They are now hitting at us from the flanks. Also, will still call you. Lt Horner.

Heavy fire was falling all over Mount Strettoia. We were shelled by huge guns, 152 or 170 mm, based about a dozen miles away at Punta Bianca on the southern tip of the Montemarcello promontory to protect the harbor at La Spezia. Company C of the 1st Battalion was now fighting alongside us; combat losses had led to overlapping commands.

Captain Brown had lost a key officer in Lieutenant Skinner and twenty other men in the disastrous fight at Seravezza. Reports came from Company L that their patrol "had been jumped upon by Germans and were wrestling with them." We took this report to be the product of someone's lively imagination rather than reality. Ten minutes later, word came that L Company was under heavy mortar and machine-gun fire. The column had broken, and a large number of men in Company L had run off. The leadership of Company L was clearly shaken, and some of the men were obviously reluctant to face barbed wire, mines, and heavy enemy fire. It was then that they began to leave the hill. Colonel Daugette went in search of Company L to reorganize the attack.

Early on October 22, Captain Pratt, 3rd Battalion operations officer, talked by radio with Lieutenant Horner. Horner said that three or four men from his forward platoon reported that the enemy was enveloping them. After talking to the Battalion CO, Captain Pratt ordered that the reserve platoon dig in, secure its flanks, and hold. Lieutenant Cox placed a mortar barrage of six hundred rounds on the enemy position in front of Horner and ended the enemy counterattack. For his efforts against eight German counterattacks that night, fighting until he and his men were out of ammunition, Horner was awarded the Silver Star for gallantry in action.

Owing to the numbers of men who had left the scene of combat, Colonel Sherman called headquarters on October 23 to say, "No strange faces are to be fed in the chow lines but are to be put under arrest instead." Those of us at battalion headquarters were receiving reports of missing men from company commanders and platoon leaders. We recorded the information and sent it to regimental headquarters. Strange faces did not show up at our mess lines.

On the 24th, Company L reported that their present strength was 146 men, down from 157, with two men killed and six wounded during the Strettoia battle. Ten men were missing and another was clearly AWOL. One of the missing soon returned. Later that morning Captain Jarman reported that he was receiving artillery fire and that some of his men had left the hill. Regimental headquarters sent MPs out to round up the stragglers. Moments later S-2 and S-1 were sent out to stop men from leaving Company I, which was also under heavy fire. Colonel Daugette left for the I Company sector to assess the situation.

During the early weeks of our 3rd Battalion combat operations, enlisted men like me were on duty at all hours in the battalion command post. There was no duty officer. Higher command noted this and ordered that an *officer* be on duty at all times. It was a sound decision because many times after a demanding day I would be very tired and sleepy while answering the phone and recording information. Once when I was on duty, Lieutenant Madison of Company I called and said a green flare had been spotted at a certain point. I recorded the information in the journal. The next day Colonel Daugette told me that the information about the flare should have been relayed to Corps Headquarters. I told him I had not received such instructions.

Enemy resistance on Mount Cauala continued throughout the day. Company I reported heavy concentrations of artillery and machine-gun fire, and for a long time no communication with the company was possible; their precise position was unknown. Company K was engaged in a firefight on Hill 101, where Captain Reedy said he had only one squad remaining of his 3rd Platoon after the rest of his men had scattered. Contact with Company I was resumed early on the morning of October 26. They had no men on the north peak of Maine after heavy shelling had caused the men to retreat. All of our units on Maine were taking artillery, mortar, machine-gun, and even grenade attacks.

Midday on October 27, Lieutenant Horner reported that his patrol had gone up Highway 1 and cut right to Alaska. Highway 1 was parallel to the coast, about two miles inland. They had found a place to blow the Germans' protective wire. As they returned, they believed they saw an enemy patrol larger than theirs moving along the road at the base of Alaska so they took cover. A second Company L patrol, under Lieutenant Hanes, set out at 1000 hours and ran into some wire, but they managed to reach an empty house. They moved up the hill and found a small dwelling filled with civilians. Continuing up the hill, they came to heavy wire that they could not get through. Rocks began falling, and the patrol descended. Company K also reported encountering heavy barbed wire.

Regimental headquarters, code name Ditto, ordered that all frontline companies send out patrols to the front until they encountered the enemy. Company L's patrol included one NCO, eight men, two Tommy guns, and one Browning automatic rifle. The patrol was to proceed to Alaska and move forward until they met the enemy. Company I went forward with one officer and twelve enlisted men, and Company K, consisting of one platoon under Lieutenant Lewis, was to proceed through Strettoia.

Early in the afternoon of October 27, we learned that the two other regiments of the 92nd Division—the 365th and 371st Infantry Regiments—were soon to bolster us and be instructed by veterans of the combat team.

On October 28, while battalion headquarters was still at Pozzi, Private Roy T. Edwards shot himself in the hand. The incident was scheduled for investigation.

Fighting on Mount Cauala continued for days with Exchanges of artillery and machine-gun fire but no lasting success on our part.

The evening of October 31 at Pozzi was clear and pleasant under moonlight. The men of the 371st and 365th Infantry Regiments began to reinforce Combat Team 370 at the front. We were no longer alone in trying to make the Germans think we were a whole division rather than a regimental combat team. Also on that date, Captain Brown and Captain Reedy arrived in the battalion command post to attend the general courts-martial of Lieutenants Butler and Noel Greenidge, two platoon leaders who had refused to engage in patrol activity against the Germans. Lieutenant Greenidge was a slim, scholarly looking Negro officer who wore glasses. He was a lonely figure as he stood outside battalion headquarters awaiting action by higher command. In January 1945 we learned that he had been sentenced to twenty-five years' hard labor. I never saw and did not know Lieutenant Butler or the sentence he received. The trials were presided over by a Colonel Osborne, and several battalion officers were called to testify. The two lieutenants may have realized that they were being asked to sacrifice their lives and the lives of their men only to continue after the war as second-class citizens. Perhaps their intent will never be known.

The severe casualties taken during the Seravezza fight and the heavy fighting on Mount Cauala caused numbers of men to drift away from combat positions. Some went to the rear lines, giving the appearance they were there on official business, but it was obvious that they were "goldbricking," just trying to get away from their assigned duty.

One of the harsh criticisms made of the Negro troops in general and of the 92nd Infantry Division in particular, was that too many lacked the will and courage to fight. They were accused of "melting away." Negro attorney Truman K. Gibson (1912–2005) used that term when he served as civilian aide to Secretary of War Henry L. Stimson during the war. Gibson's role was created by President Franklin Delano Roosevelt so that Negroes would have a spokesman in the U.S. Army.

Gibson used "melting away" to describe the "disappearance" of combat soldiers from the front; that is, their avoidance of combat. The enlisted men I served alongside used a different phrase: they said they had "unassed the hill." The phrase was not entirely derogatory because when men were being fired upon or faced superior power, they got back under cover. That is what *our* phrase meant. I believe Gibson was talking about men who just walked out of the combat zone. The phenomenon is as old as men at war: in my recent reading I encountered the phrase "melting away" to describe desertions in the battles between the Spartans and the Athenians 2,500 years ago.

The fact is that we failed, despite several efforts, to take and control Mount Cauala and, later, the city of Massa. Failure has widely been attributed to the unwillingness of Negro troops to stand and fight. Daniel K. Gibran, author of *The 92nd Infantry Division and the Italian Campaign in World War II* (McFarland & Co., Inc., 2001, ISBN-13:978-0-7864-1009-3), quotes Lieutenant Robt. D. Montjoy, Negro commander of Company C, 370th Infantry, as saying of Negro troops after a fourth attempt to capture Mount Cauala (p. 57): "They will not stay in their positions unless constantly watched and give as their reason for leaving the fact that the men next to them will leave anyway so there is no reason for them to stay. . . .The few good officers and non-commissioned officers in the company are not able to carry the load placed on them, no matter how hard they work. Morale is bad and I dread to make a night move, because so many of the men can slip away." General Almond is reported to have said that the men "lacked the guts to fight with tenacity and determination." My response to those comments is that officers and platoon leaders were being killed and wounded trying to lead men who all their lives had been treated as second-class citizens. Those same men and their children displayed plenty of determination and guts during the later civil-rights marches, sit-ins, and in subsequent wars when military segregation was history.

Lieutenant Colonel John Phelan, charismatic and athletic executive officer of the 370th Infantry Regiment, reported on

October 13 (Gibran, p. 58): "During my period of observation, I have heard of just as many acts of individual heroism among Negro troops as among white. There is no reason to believe that there is any greater lack of individual guts among them." Gibran cites Phelan's statement, which now is part of the 92nd Division files in the National Archives at Suitland, Maryland.

Phelan did add, however, the following: "On the other hand, the tendency to mass hysteria or panic is much more prevalent among colored troops." As he moved about the combat team's front, helping battalion and company commanders get their men started back up first one slope and then another, first across one creek and then another, he felt that he had gathered enough impressions to support this point of view. However, the basis for the tendency to panic was not understood. Later explanations on the grounds of low test scores and poor motivation did not bear close examination. A simpler explanation was a lack of trust, beginning during training.

Phelan, incidentally, was killed in action during the last campaign of the war in Italy. I heard that he was trying to assist another regiment that had been assigned to the 92nd Division.

During my participation in the Italian campaign, I never witnessed any mass hysteria or panic. I was among the men many times when we were shot at or blasted by heavy artillery. We were all pretty stoic and accepted the way things were in combat. I do believe that some of the men had lively imaginations and were inventive in describing things that never happened, and it is possible that the coded language used by Negro soldiers to confuse the white man was wrongly interpreted by higher-ups. At the same time, I know that the enlisted men did adopt various strategies to avoid being killed. The attacks that we made were in rugged mountain country. Our men were not out in the open where they could be seen all the time. You hid behind a rock, a tree, or a destroyed building to avoid being shot. When you are attacking from the sea, as at Normandy or Iwo Jima, there is nowhere to duck. You move forward or die. In mountainous country it is very easy to lose contact with your leader, and when the leader is wounded or killed—as was the case many times—confusion reigns. Too many times our men were isolated without leadership and with no knowledge of the objective. Also, there was in many of their minds the belief that they were "being screwed" by being on that mission in the first place.

After the war, Truman Gibson was the only Negro member of President Harry S. Truman's advisory committee on military training, and it was during Gibson's term of service, specifically in 1948, that Truman ordered an end to segregation in the army. I knew Gibson and spoke with him on at least one occasion after the war; his family was prominently involved in the life insurance business in Chicago as mine was in Los Angeles. His ultimate contribution to the welfare of the Negro fighting man strengthened America and helped make the nation fairer to all its citizens.

As November approached, the 92nd Division's newly arrived 371st Regiment was ordered to relieve the 3rd Battalion and we were to move to Barga, a small town to the northeast, where we were to replace a Brazilian unit. Thirty trucks were coming to transport us at 1000 hours the next morning.

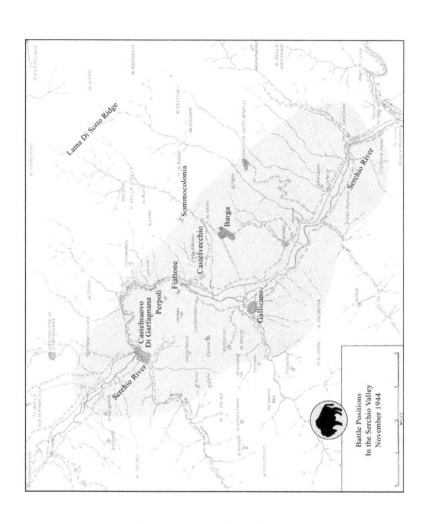

Lama Di Sotto Ridge

Serchio River

Sommocolonia

Barga

Castelvecchio

Fiattone

Perpoli

Castelnuovo
Di Garfagnana

Gallicano

Serchio River

Battle Positions
In the Serchio Valley
November 1944

MILES

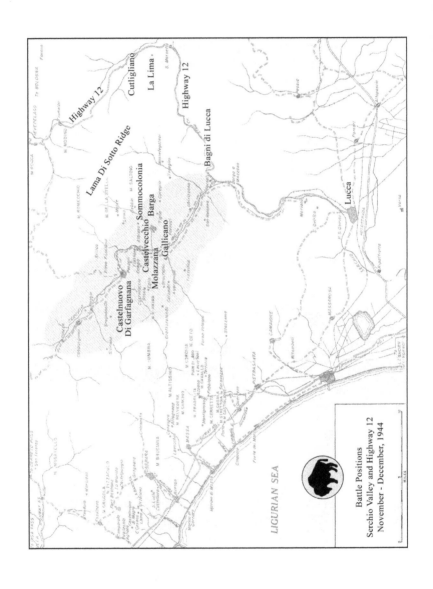

Battle Positions
Serchio Valley and Highway 12
November - December, 1944

NOVEMBER

November 3, 1944, arrived with thunder and the threat of rain. Promptly at 1000 hours the battalion moved out. A new command post was established 2.3 miles south of Pietrasanta. The 3rd Battalion was to relieve the 7th and 8th companies of the Brazilian Expeditionary Force (also known as the FEB) in the Serchio Valley near Barga at 1900 hours.

November 4 marked the dissolution of Combat Team 370 as the advance unit of the 92nd Infantry Division. Colonel R. G. Sherman took note of the event with the issuance of General Orders Number 81, which should serve in part to answer critics who found Negro troops en masse wanting in courage. I am proud to include it here:

As this Combat Team passes into history, I, who have had the privilege of commanding it, desire to review, with you, some of the high lights of its brief, but extremely active life.

Consisting of selected officers and men, this Combat Team was designated for immediate combat duty in an active theater and sailed from the United States, 15 July 1944, for the Italian Theater. In addition to its Combat Mission, Combat Team 370 was charged with the duty of preparing the way for the remainder of the 92nd Infantry Division, soon to follow in our footsteps.

Three weeks after landing in Italy, Combat Team 370, then a member of the famous Fifth Army, found itself fighting at the front as a team-mate of the old and experienced First Armored Division. Never have two units worked more in harmony or with better results—across the Arno River—over Mount Pisano—into the Gothic Line defenses near Bagni di Lucca—armor, infantry and artillery, each assisting the other, while their respective supply units, also working together, kept the assault echelons well cared for in food, ammunition and other essentials to combat.

From the Serchio River Valley, Combat Team 370 moved to the Montecatini sector and drove forward into the Gothic Line defenses north of Cutigliano. Later it was shifted to the west to take its place in the drive toward Massa.

Upon the arrival of the remainder of the 92nd Division, Combat Team 370 was dissolved after 73 days of continual action against the enemy. During this time it advanced over 50 miles.

An advance by any troops, against enemy resistance, cannot be made without cost, and the Combat Team has paid such cost willingly, because it was necessary in defeating our enemy. Many officers and enlisted men of Combat Team 370 were killed, wounded or missing in action. Let each one of us gratefully remember those who have given their all that we might carry on.

How well Combat Team 370 carried out its mission of preparing the way for the remainder of the division can best be told by the fact that the Combat Team was commended by the city of Richmond, Virginia, for its fine conduct and appearance while on pass. The Military Police of the Combat Team were highly commended by the Police officials of Richmond, Virginia, for their superior performance of duty while the Combat Team was on leave there. The Combat Team was again commended by the Port of Embarkation for its discipline, fine spirit and soldierly conduct while staging at Patrick Henry, Virginia. Again after crossing the Atlantic it was commended for its discipline and conduct and the fact that the ships used were kept in a superior state of police throughout the entire voyage. At the staging area in Naples, the Combat Team was commended by Lieutenant General Devers for its discipline and fine appearance, and again, upon relief from attachment to the First Armored Division after over a month together in combat, the Combat Team was commended for its teamwork and cooperation and combat efficiency.

The record made by Combat Team 370 is enviable and is one to which we, as the first colored Combat Team in the European Theater, can well point with pride.

As commander of Combat Team 370, I desire to commend and thank all members of the Combat Team for their individual and collective efforts which made this fine record possible.

You now will return to your original assignments within the 92nd Infantry Division, better men because of the knowledge of a duty well done, and better men because you have experience which will benefit the remainder of the division. Use your knowledge and experience well and exert every effort to bringing all members of the division to that standard of proficiency which you personally know by experience to be necessary to successful combat against the enemy.

May God bless you and keep you and help you through the tasks facing us. Remember Combat Team 370 and keep its standards which yourself set and lived up to so successfully.

R. G. Sherman

Colonel, Infantry

Commanding

Colonel Sherman was clearly proud of the achievements of Combat Team 370. He knew that we were green when we went into battle. He knew that many of our enlisted men did not meet army standards. And he also knew that we fought as hard as we could at Seravezza, where there were no trained reserves to replace our casualties. Within the combat team there were few soldiers ready to assume leadership roles when officers and noncommissioned officers became casualties. I believe Sherman's order was an honest expression of his sentiments.

On November 4, we were on the eastern flank of the 92nd Division, in the Serchio River Valley, fifteen miles east of Barga and Gallicano. We traveled by army truck at night. To the west was the 371st Infantry and on their left, bordering the Ligurian Sea, was the 2nd Armored Group. Company I was stationed north of Barga along the Serchio; Company K held a center position toward Sommocolonia; and L Company was on the right, north of Sommocolonia.

The Division command post was established at Viareggio "under canvas and in vans next to the Principe de Piemonte Hotel, with most officers billeted in the hotel," according to Colonel St. John Arnold (p. 43), who adds in *Buffalo Soldiers* that the general's mess was established in a casino across the street, where the 92nd Division Band "played soft dinner music each evening" and jazz after General Almond had left the dinner table. We never knew of a division band and certainly never had music with our meals. During all our time in combat, I don't recall going to see any entertainment, although I understand that every now and then a USO team would show up to perform; and sometimes the men were sent back to see a Hollywood movie.

On November 5, 3rd Battalion moved into Barga, east of the Serchio River, and began patrolling to determine enemy positions. It was near Barga that Alejandro, or Alexander, Novani joined the 3rd Battalion. He was a sixteen-year-old Italian partisan who had been raised in England and had a British accent. Alexander was a tall, light-skinned northern Italian, an average-looking young man. He served as battalion interpreter and was especially useful when we had contact with Italian partisans who were fighting with us. We usually called him "Paisano." He ate and slept with us for several months and readily picked up American Negro slang from the troops and pounds from eating in our chow lines. Alexander usually rode in Lieutenant Harrington's jeep because Harrington, our intelligence officer, was always in touch with and talking to the partisan leader in the area we occupied. The antifascist partisans would tell us what was going on. They would help us when we needed help, but mostly they were engaged in their own operations against the Germans. The Germans were fierce with any partisans they captured and would shoot them on sight. In appearance the partisans were a bedraggled lot, dressed in ratty old clothes. Most wore red scarves, which made for easy identification.

Task Force 92 was dissolved on November 6, and the 92nd Division came under the direct control of the Fifth Army. The division's mission was to command the coastal area, a twenty-mile-wide line between Barga and the sea.

On November 7 at 2000 hours, a Company I patrol went to San Pietro in Campo, where a civilian had reported that an Alpine lieutenant (Italian Alpine Troops fought with the Germans) and two enlisted men had left town a few hours earlier. The I Company patrol moved on to Castelvecchio, where they questioned civilians and learned that an enemy patrol had indeed gone through town and proceeded to Santa Maria Quirico. Civilians led the patrol to a house where they were able to see to C. Bechelli and vicinity. The patrol spotted two machine-gun positions and two mortar positions. There were approximately one hundred Italian troops in a draw north of Santa Maria Quirico and a platoon of Germans in the vicinity of Fiattone. North at Perpoli there was reported to be a battalion of Germans. All footpaths and trails in the vicinity of Santa Maria Quirico were mined. The area was the site of limited action.

During this threatening time, General Almond expressed his displeasure when he learned that Captain Jarman was on leave in Rome. His response to the news was to order that at no time could officers occupying frontline positions leave those positions without permission from the battalion commander. Almond's pronouncements went out to all companies. At the same time, division and regiment staff officers expressed concern that front-line platoon leaders were visiting rear areas while their platoons were in frontline positions. It should be noted that all division and regimental staff officers were White and mostly Southern, and almost all platoon leaders were Negroes. To the reader it must appear, with all of these departures and ramblings, that things were disorganized and even chaotic. Very often they were.

On November 11, a Company I patrol under Lieutenant Martin left at 0115 hours, passed through San Pietro in Campo, turned left, crossed the Corsonna River, and went along the bank approximately three hundred yards, passing to the west of Castelvecchio. A partisan there told the patrol of a route that had no mines but was covered by machine-gun fire. He stated that there were mines to the left of the path, so it was decided to go up the path as far as possible. It was so close to enemy gun emplacements that it was impossible for the engineering officer to use mine detectors. After deploying men to cover their advance, the patrol moved only about 150 yards before hand grenades began being thrown at the patrol. It was impossible to move quietly because of fallen leaves. The partisan guided the patrol through another path that he thought was mined. The engineering officer swept all the way up the path to a draw. At that point, the Germans again threw grenades at the patrol. The minefields were nothing new. The Germans used barbed wire and minefields all along the front lines and crisscrossed the minefields with machine-gun fire. That afternoon all company clerks and the battalion sergeant majors moved to Viareggio, the 92nd Division's headquarters, to form a personnel section.

Just before 1800 on November 11, men of Company I learned that a German officer and two enlisted men came to Castelvecchio every night to eat. Captain Jarman, just back from his Roman holiday, sent a patrol of five men to bolster the patrol already in the town and see if the Germans could be ambushed. Upon entering a house that they had chosen as an observation point, and which they assumed was vacant, the patrol was fired upon from within the house. Two men were reported probably dead and another as seriously wounded. One man returned. Captain Jarman was attempting to evacuate the two men reported as "probably dead."

The two Company I soldiers who had indeed been killed that day were Sergeant McKinley B. Scott and Private George E. Gray. I had spent quite a lot of time with both men when we crossed the Atlantic on the *Mariposa*. We had played cards together with Sergeant James E. Reid, who had been the first in our division to die shortly after we entered combat in August. Now three members of our card-playing group were dead. Reid was probably thirty years old, while Scott and Gray, both from the Army Specialized Training Program (ASTP), were only nineteen. My age. I had last seen Mac Scott when we prepared for a German counterattack at Seravezza. We were both in the kitchen of a vacated house that had been partially destroyed. A large piece of shrapnel was lying on the kitchen table. It must have fallen there during an explosion.

Later, Company I filed a more detailed patrol report on the deaths of Scott and Gray. Those two and a third enlisted man had presumably been guided to that house by a friendly Italian who had visited with the company quite often. As they approached the house, a machine gun opened up from inside, killing Scott and Gray. The third enlisted man, Duberry, escaped with a wounded wrist. He returned to the company and reported that the Italian guide had been killed alongside Scott and Gray.

A subsequent patrol sent out to investigate further provided still more specific details on the ambush. They established that one Italian officer and two enlisted men had been reported eating in a house in Castelvecchio. Company I's patrol, including Duberry, Scott, and Gray, had proceeded to that house. Now, as the second investigating patrol approached the house where Scott and Gray had been killed, they saw the Italian "guide" standing unharmed in the doorway. Wounded enlisted man Duberry added later that the Italian who had led the patrol into the ambush had come to the company and talked with Lieutenant Martin and then departed. He returned to the house from which the patrol had been observing German activity in time to lead the patrol to his house. He had said that there were no enemy soldiers in town. He entered the house first. An automatic weapon then had opened up, killing Scott and Gray and wounding Duberry. It had been a setup.

I learned of the deaths of Scott and Gray because one of my duties was to report casualties to regimental headquarters each night. I was deeply affected, absolutely stunned, by the ambush killing of Mac Scott and George Gray, two men I had known, and I did not share the news with our friends for two or three days. Some of my friends in intelligence were upset with me because I failed to report the deaths immediately. I guess I did not want to be the bearer of bad news.

At 0950 the next morning, Company I reported that the Italian "guide" was being questioned. According to his story, the men who fired on the patrol had fired from *outside* the house and not from within as we had been led to believe. He was turned over to partisan headquarters for further questioning. The bodies of Scott and Gray were found where the ambush occurred.

Men who were killed in action and could be identified became the responsibility of Lieutenant Grayson, the regiment's Graves Registration Officer. His responsibility was to arrange for temporary burial. There would be every effort to identify the body and to send it back to temporary burial sites well behind the lines. Later those men who had died in action were gathered and their burial place became the U.S. Military Cemetery in Florence. Today, as I have mentioned, that cemetery honors 4,402 soldiers, sailors, and airmen. I have been there three times, most recently in 2002. Few places I know of are more beautiful than Tuscany, and in a tiny corner of that stunning region of Italy lie four hundred Black Americans, descendants of slaves, who marched, fought, and died fighting and defeating the great evil of Nazi Germany. The blood of Buffalo Soldiers mingles in historic soil with the blood of the ancient Romans. The names of another 1,409 men fill a Wall of the Missing. One of them was the last Black infantry officer killed during our tenure in combat. Why his body is listed as missing in action, I don't know. That was Lieutenant John M. Madison from Company I, winner of the Silver Star, Bronze Star, and Purple Heart. He is listed on the wall as missing in action, yet he appears in our battalion journal as wounded and then killed on April 5, 1945.

Telephone communication in early November 1944 was disrupted by German artillery and mortar fire. Wire chief Sergeant Joseph reported that new lines had to be laid to all companies. A preacher, Sergeant Joseph would take his men out to repair the lines during heavy shelling. They would sing Negro spirituals during the bombardment as they repaired the lines. None of Sergeant Joseph's men was ever wounded. Joseph carried a rifle but vowed never to use it. He was an inspirational leader.

Barga, on the Serchio River north of Lucca, was a hotbed of activity in November. German and American soldiers interacted with Italian partisans and civilians. Each of our companies had partisans attached. Some could speak English, and most knew the territory. We had discovered that there were Russians serving in the German army and other Russians attempting to escape after having served with the Germans. These turncoats would often cross the front lines seeking to ally themselves with the Americans.

Snow had begun falling on the mountains, and it grew very cold. It was clear that winter was coming. One night I was moving up, among a column of soldiers, when a halt was called as we were near a shed. Someone found some charcoal and started a fire in the shed. We all sat and lay down to rest, and it was not long before we grew drowsy. Captain Shires came along, opened the shed, and found us there—all of us falling asleep. He kicked out the fire and said that it would not have been long before all of us were dead.

On November 15, Captain Reedy of Company K received a report from a civilian who said he had learned from a German soldier that the Germans were planning to attack Barga with three battalions. The attack did not come until December; but in the meantime, in the mid-November fighting, men would frequently lag behind in an attack. By the time an objective was reached, *if* it was reached, they would be nowhere in sight. In their own words, they had "unassed the hill," and it was they who contributed further to the continuing charges of "melting away" that were leveled at the 92nd Division. Most of the missing men did finally turn up; they had been stragglers who purposely lost contact with the rest of the men.

Most of our troops were anything but stragglers. I learned only after the war that Lieutenant Magellan C. Mars, company commander of the 371st Infantry Regiment's Company K, had been killed by machine-gun fire and half his company killed or wounded following an intense mortar attack on November 17. For his gallantry in protecting his men, Lieutenant Mars earned a posthumous Silver Star. As a boy of about twelve, I had attended

YMCA Camp in Los Angeles, where one of our counselors was Magellan C. Mars. He was a great guy, then in his early twenties. We had called him "Crip."

On November 17, the battalion commander called Captains Brown, Reedy, and Jarman and told each to send out a platoon and advance as far as possible toward Lama di Soto and Castelvecchio, to dig in and hold. That day, Colonel Sherman ordered the battalion to keep the enemy busy on our side of the river.

Company I reported that their platoon was receiving heavy artillery fire. K Company's platoon and patrol reported that one mortar round had fallen short, wounding the platoon sergeant, an enlisted man, and the forward observer. More "friendly fire." Then at 1455 hours Company K reported that everybody was off the hill and back to the same line they had occupied on November 15.

At 1655 hours, Company L reported that fifteen Black Shirts—Italian Fascists—had attacked on the left front and that one soldier was killed and one was missing.

Our operations just to the north of Barga were receiving much resistance from the Germans and from the Italian Fascists. After these patrols, which did establish that the enemy was still resisting, our men returned to their original line of departure. All during the day, the men had encountered numerous minefields, and a great deal of artillery fire and machine-gun fire could be heard around Barga. Artillery and mortar fire from far above had kept the 3rd Battalion from reaching Lama, just north of Sommocolonia.

Jake McInnis, who had been a hero at Seravezza with his Browning automatic rifle, was ordered to division headquarters to receive his Silver Star.

On the morning of November 18, some men who had refused to go on the previous day's mission were brought in under arrest and sent to the rear. Most of these men were back in their company the next day.

Captain Reedy reported that the so-called Mule Skinners, the four-company 92nd Division Pack Battalion under the command of Lieutenant Hugh Hanley, which used local Italians and Italian mules to transport rations and ammunitions to our troops, were complaining about receiving C-rations instead of what our troops were given, which were K-rations. I am not sure there was a significant difference in quality. C-rations consisted of six cans that included an entrée such as canned beans, canned hash, or canned stew, cheese, crackers, candy, a canned dessert, and an accessory pack made up of a can opener, mix for a hot beverage, salt and sugar packets, plastic spoon, chewing gum, a pack of four cigarettes, and several sheets of toilet paper. Each complete meal provided approximately 1,200 calories.

The K-ration was an individual daily combat food ration intended to last for a day and provided three meals: breakfast, dinner (lunch), and supper. Breakfast consisted of canned meat and eggs, a fruit bar, and instant coffee. Lunch was canned cheese and a lemon, orange, or grape drink packet. The dinner packet package contained toilet paper, a bouillon pack, and a lemon, orange, or grape drink packet. The three meals provided about three thousand calories. (The K-ration was produced by the Cracker Jack Company, and the K-ration box was about the same size as a Cracker Jack box.)

At 1010 two squads led by Lieutenant Hailstork of L Company left the company command post. Captain Brown had threatened to kill one man before and now gave instructions to the section leader to shoot any man who tried to ignore orders. He also instructed his outposts to shoot any man who returned from the combat zone before he was ordered to do so. In order to leave a combat zone, a platoon leader would have to receive approval from company and battalion superior officers. Captain Reedy's patrol returned and reported that one soldier was killed and three were wounded. Company I's and Company L's patrols were still out at 1445 hours. The battalion was instructed by regimental headquarters to continue sending out daily patrols day and night.

On November 19, the weather was clear and cold. We were still in our command post at Barga. At 1629 hours, the battalion outpost reported enemy propaganda leaflets falling on our side of the line. Our intelligence officer called the companies and asked that someone bring in one of the leaflets. Intended to lower our morale, the leaflets were delivered by artillery or dropped from German planes. We returned the favor: Division Intelligence authorized the use of C- or K-rations for the purpose of enticing Italian Republic soldiers to desert. Propaganda leaflets advertising the availability of food were to be distributed to the Germans by the partisans, if possible.

November 20 was cloudy and cool. At 1008 hours, the Ammunition and Pioneer Platoon reported holding two Italians who had fled from the Germans, and they were wondering what to do with them. At 1045 Lieutenant Davis of Company L reported that he had encountered sixty partisans and some American flyers coming from behind the lines. They had been in a firefight with the Germans. Some were wounded. Five minutes later Colonel Daugette reported that 270 people from across the lines were on their way to our command post. At 1215 hours, American Air Force officers and enlisted men arrived. They had been prisoners of war who had escaped from the enemy and made their way across the lines. They were promptly sent to the rear. None who surrendered or who had escaped ever stayed with us.

We were notified that the Division's Buffalo Soldier shoulder patches had arrived and were to be put on our uniforms. From our arrival in Italy in August until November 20, we had not worn our buffalo patches nor anything else that identified the unit we represented. That lack of identification was obviously meant to confuse the Germans, but Axis Sally had known who we were from the day we arrived in Italy.

On November 21, we were told that we were free to fire at any plane coming in under six thousand feet. Later, Regimental headquarters changed the orders, and we learned that we were free to fire on all planes under *three thousand* feet. At 1440 hours on November 22, our outposts reported that four of our planes had strafed Castelnuovo, north of our position. Later that evening our instructions were altered once more: under Fifth Army orders, we were not to fire on *any* planes unless attacked.

On November 23, Thanksgiving Day, at 1145 hours, our field kitchens were provided with turkey, and our chaplain visited all companies. Battalion Chaplain Hubert Jones regularly held services and was always available to any soldier who wished to discuss any personal problem. Chaplain Jones was based in the 3rd Battalion Headquarters Company and reported to Colonel Daugette. We had a joke that after anyone shared his problem(s) with the chaplain, he would receive a "TS" card, meaning "Tough Shit." The truth is that Chaplain Jones was a very fine officer, and his presence meant a lot to the men.

The next morning was hazy and not too cool. At 0225 hours, Regimental Operations reported that the password had been used over the telephone—an act that was forbidden. The password was not changed at that time, but all units were alerted to double-check those persons using the password. At 0715 hours, L Company reported that its patrol had made it three-quarters of the way up the ridge to the town of Lama di Sotto. A white flare went up in the vicinity of the trees to the right of the houses there. Soon a machine gun was heard coming from a position in front of the houses. L Company's patrol backed down the ridge and discovered that the firing was coming from partisans shooting at a small German patrol. Two hours later, the A&P platoon brought three prisoners to the command post. A partisan woman had brought them through the lines to the A&P position. At 1620 hours that afternoon, Regiment called to order that the battalion occupy the line with two companies, with the third to rest in reserve. Another order mandated that every man turn in a pair of dirty socks before dinner. The army and Division Headquarters were concerned about trench foot, which resulted from people wearing damp socks in damp shoes for prolonged periods. The condition could lead to tissue loss and eventually require amputation. We were all eager to comply. At 1842 hours, battalion Intelligence called Regimental Operations and said that partisan headquarters reported the enemy blowing up everything in Castelnuovo and moving back to Villa Colle Mondina.

Day and night patrols continued on November 25, a cloudy, misty day. Nothing of significance happened. The next day Captain Shires left Barga on a pass for Florence. An officer could go on leave as long as he obtained his superior officer's permission. We experienced the usual amount of shelling from the enemy throughout the day.

At 2100 hours our supply officer, Lieutenant Oxley, was in the command post. He reported that each of our companies now had nine BARs and eleven Tommy guns. We took this as evidence that the Fifth Army realized that its riflemen were being outgunned by the enemy's burp guns and were increasing the number of automatic weapons for each rifle company.

Patrolling continued on November 27, and Company L's platoon reached Sommocolonia, where it was pinned down. Lieutenant Horner reported that he had only seven men left. Captain Brown, L Company commander, reported to Colonel Daugette that a machine gun had opened up on Horner's left flank but had been silenced by our .50-caliber machine guns.

Then another machine gun, supplemented by mortar fire, began firing on L Company's position.

On the morning of November 28, a platoon leader of Company L reported that twenty men in one of the company's rifle platoons and an additional five with light machine guns had fired at enemy sighted in Lama di Sotto. A sniper began firing back, and when the platoon leader next checked he had only five men left; the others had run off. Other patrols of L Company were proceeding up a slope to Lama di Sotto. Civilians reported that the Germans near Lama di Sotto were laying shoe mines. Later that morning, Captain Jarman reported that six of his men and two civilians had been wounded and evacuated. Mortar fire was everywhere.

In the last days of November, the 366th Infantry Regiment, with all Negro officers and enlisted men, was attached to the 92nd Division. They had been in Italy since May, serving as security troops for the Air Force. Now they were thrust into combat with less than adequate training. It was reported by men in the regiment that General Almond made clear during his opening address to the 366th his unhappiness over their attachment to the division. The 366th Regiment was under the command of Colonel Howard D. Queen, who had led them since 1943 and was apparently much respected by his men. On December 15, just two weeks after the attachment, Colonel Queen asked to be relieved of his command on the grounds that the treatment he and his men had received "has been such as to disturb me mentally and has not been such as is usually given an officer of my grade and service." Queen said he wished "to keep my record clear and up to normal expectations, before I break under the present strain as I am now physically and mentally exhausted" (Lee, p. 559). Queen was relieved by Lieutenant Colonel Alonzo Ferguson, his executive officer.

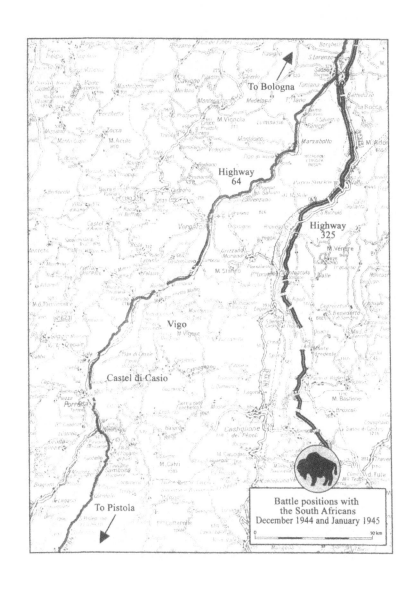

**Battle positions with
the South Africans
December 1944 and January 1945**

0   10 km

DECEMBER

The early days of December were clear and cold. Third Battalion was ordered almost thirty miles east and attached to the 6th South African Armored Division's 11th Armored Brigade at Castel di Casio. This sector was deep in the Apennines, northwest of Florence and north of Pistoia along Highway 64. The South Africans had fought with the British Eighth Army and defeated Field Marshal Erwin Rommel's Afrika Korps in the North African desert in 1943. We remained alongside the South Africans through December and January. At first we were housed in a castle, but we later moved to a small factory and then to a farmhouse in the mountains.

On December 6, Captain Reedy, company commander of K Company, was ordered to regimental headquarters to act as intelligence officer while one of the headquarters personnel was attending school. Lieutenant Brackett, a White officer in K Company, was placed in command of Company L.

That night we received a message sent to all companies ordering the men to cease killing chickens because of a complaint from the civilian population.

On December 7, a misty and chilly day, our battalion officers visited the headquarters of the 11th South African Armored Brigade and discussed our battalion's relief of one of their battalions in line. As our companies were getting into position to relieve the South Africans, they had to pass over a bridge in sight of German guns. We had to create a smoky atmosphere so that the bridge was obscured in order to avoid German fire at the crossing. We were now operating under command of the South Africans. Their procedures were slightly different from ours. For example, we no longer called in at night to report our situation. Instead, they called us at first light to get our status report. Our patrols continued to go out on schedule, but there was nothing to report. Headquarters moved to a large farmhouse south of Riola, seven miles north of Castel di Casio and even deeper into the mountains. A South African liaison officer, Captain West, was with us. The men of the armored brigade were all White South Africans, mainly from the English part of South Africa. The officers had Black orderlies who made their beds and ran errands for them. When asked by Colonel Daugette what the population of South Africa was, the liaison officer said, "Three million White and seven million Black South Africans."

General Mark Clark left the Fifth Army on December 16 to take command of the 15th Army Group and was succeeded by Lieutenant General Lucian K. Truscott Jr. In other words, Clark now commanded all Allied armies in Italy while Truscott commanded the Fifth Army.

We learned that day that Lieutenant Isaac Jones of Company I had been killed by friendly fire, but we heard no further details.

The 3rd Battalion was now operating alongside Brazilians and South Africans as part of an international force.

On December 23, we saw the first heavy snow cover the North Apennines, and the air was cold and windy. Some of our troops were issued white snow uniforms. It seemed unreal to me that Negro troops from the American South were wearing snow-white uniforms and fighting in ten-foot-deep snowdrifts.

One of the soldiers standing guard in the snow outside battalion headquarters was Hiram MacBeth, the Southern farm boy who had slept when we were being fired upon after we had crossed the Arno. MacBeth looked very cold in his white snow uniform. I had written home to my grandmother in October, telling her that the weather was beginning to grow cold and we had not been issued warm clothing. I received from her in December a woolen sleeveless sweater that she had knitted in army olive drab. It felt great. She included with the sweater one of her special fruitcakes, laced with spirits and wrapped carefully in cloth. I shared the cake with my friend at headquarters on Christmas Day 1944.

From our position thirty miles to the east, along Highway 64 leading to Bologna, we learned that the Germans had attacked our division before dawn on December 26 at several points on a six-mile front along the Serchio River. The 1st Battalion of the 370th Infantry, 92nd Division, was pounded by heavy machinegun fire near Molazzana, and elements of the 2nd Battalion were struck equally hard near Calomini, nearby. The village of Sommocolonia was being held by two platoons of the 366th Infantry's E Company, which was soon engaged in fighting door-to-door and hand-to-hand with German foot troops.

Twenty-six-year-old Lieutenant John R. Fox, an artillery observer with the 366th Infantry's Cannon Company, was killed that day after calling down artillery fire on his observation post, the second floor of a house in Sommocolonia, during a German attack. The 366th Infantry was the regiment commanded by all-Negro officers that General Almond did not want to accept into the 92nd Division. Fox was recommended for the Distinguished Service Cross at the time but his widow did not receive it until May 15, 1982—thirty eight years later! The posthumous citation noted that his body was found among those of "approximately 100 German soldiers." Another fifteen years passed before President Bill Clinton awarded him the Medal of Honor.

On the day following Fox's gallant action, we received word that Barga, which had been our headquarters for quite a while, and Noce, which had been our temporary battalion headquarters, had fallen to the Germans. Two brigades of the 8th British Indian division—the motorized 19th and 21st—which had been in reserve and were now attached to the 370th Infantry, counterattacked. And within two days they pushed the enemy out of Barga and, with strong air support, retook the area around Lucca, obliterating any German threat to the Fifth Army supply line.

During the month of December, the 92nd Division captured 636 prisoners of war and had 529 of its own killed, wounded, or missing in action. While all of the action was taking place around Barga and in the Serchio Valley, we continued, while under command of the South Africans, to enjoy relative peace, except for artillery fire.

JANUARY 1945

January 1, 1945, was a memorable day in battalion headquarters. Snow was everywhere and it was very cold. Someone in Battalion Headquarters Company had been given a bottle of grappa, a powerful, clear Italian brandy distilled from grape skins, stems, and seeds. Three of us in the company had been told that we were to go over to Vigo, south of Highway 64 and about ten miles down winding roads from our Riola headquarters. There, an Italian family that had been given a turkey was going to prepare it for us. Before we left we drank the grappa and became quite high—so high, in fact, that on the trip in an open jeep over to Vigo I tossed a few grenades into the snow from my position in the rear seat. The three of us had a fine dinner served by an older Italian woman in a small house. The meal was the best I had had since leaving the States. We returned quietly to headquarters around midnight.

Days later I was given a three-day pass to Florence. Our battalion was based just north of the city, and I was able to get transportation in an army truck for the fifty-mile haul over winding mountain passes that eventually led south to Florence. In that beautiful city, enlisted men stayed at the railroad station, where bunks were set up for us. There was no segregation, and we bunked with troops of all races who were on leave from the front. Florence was very quiet. The winter streets were bare. All of the great art that was portable had been moved out by the

Italians. For example, Michelangelo's *David* was nowhere to be seen. We visited the Duomo, the great cathedral of Florence, and walked the Ponte Vecchio, the medieval bridge across the Arno that the Germans had not destroyed during their retreat in August 1944. After three cold days in Florence, I returned to our headquarters. The snow there had piled up even more than before I left. We continued patrolling, and the Germans continued firing artillery and propaganda leaflets at us. Machine-gun fire was a constant, every day and every night. However, there were very few casualties.

On or about January 13, Colonel Daugette returned from a ten-day pass to Cairo, Egypt. He flew to Cairo on a C-47 transport plane and told us he had a great time viewing the Pyramids and the Sphinx. The army provided first-class tours to famous places to its top commanders and staff officers. Junior officers and even enlisted men went to some of the famous sites. Rome was a destination even as the fighting raged. When the war ended, there were tours to Athens, Switzerland, Paris, and the French Riviera. Our battalion was relieved in line at Riola by the 81st Reconnaissance Squadron. I was one of the last persons to leave battalion headquarters and was picked up by one of the motor pool jeeps. We had a long, cold drive along icy roads, and at one point, while crossing a bridge, our jeep spun out of control and went over the side. Some Italians helped us pull the jeep out of the snow; we got back onto the road and continued fifty miles west toward Viareggio. Headquarters had been moved to an area just about two miles south of that city on the shores of the Ligurian Sea. Our battalion's stay with the South Africans had been rather uneventful except for the tragic death of Lieutenant Jones, killed by friendly fire.

Very few of us Negro troops, no matter where in the States we had come from, had experienced the kind of weather that we found in the North Apennines—snow in great deep drifts, wind, cold rain, and generally miserable weather conditions. We were actually almost as far north as Minneapolis, Minnesota, yet this was "sunny" Italy. We were glad to be back on flat ground in and around Viareggio, but we really did not know what lay ahead: Our commanding officers were planning a winter attack on the plains north of the city. While we remained near Viareggio, there were dental inspections and examinations for trench foot. Typhoid and tetanus vaccinations were given to all the men. During the inspections by the general staff, the 81-mm mortar platoon of M Company, commanded by 1st Lieutenant Harry Cox of San Mateo, California, was given an excellent rating. Lieutenant Cox's father had served with my father in the 92nd Division during World War I. After the war in Italy ended and we were still in Italy, I gave the battalion journal to then-Captain Cox for review. We became separated, and I lost contact with the journal until I met Cox some time later in San Francisco. He still had the journal, and I made copies for each of us. His copy was later lost in a fire.

In late January 1945, the weather was quite variable at Viareggio. Some days were clear and warm, others clear but cold; and still others, rainy. Third Battalion reported to Regiment that of the 147 days that we had spent on line, 132 had been spent in combat and only 15 in reserve. In January the 92nd Division took 166 prisoners.

Paul Goodman reports in *A Fragment of Victory* (p. 80) that "Of the 18.3 miles of front held by the 92nd Division throughout most of its operational period, 13.5 miles were over extremely mountainous terrain crossed only by narrow winding paths. Nearly all of the vehicles going from one front to another had to follow a circuitous 'U-shaped' route that began at Pietrasanta and went southward to Camaiore, then to Lucca, then north to Barga and Gallicano. A thirty-mile trip was necessary in order to pass from two points that were only a little over ten miles apart on the map." He says that this problem had led, back on November 17, to the formation of the 92nd Division's Mule Pack Battalion, with 1st Lieutenant Hugh B. Hanley, a cavalry officer, appointed to command it. Also, Goodman says, at its peak, the battalion included an American officer and 15 enlisted men, 600 Italian men, 372 mules, and 173 horses. I knew of the mule train but knew nothing of its organization or numbers at the time.

FEBRUARY

On February 2, a rainy day, we were still south of Viareggio in the reserve area. General Almond inspected us.

We had been in tents for just a day or two when one morning we heard rifle shots fired nearby just after we woke up. When I asked, "What the heck happened?" one of the guys told me that Private Abraham Small of Company K had shot and killed his tentmate, described by some of the men as "his old lady," after a bitter argument. I was nineteen and had never heard the term "old lady" used in that context. I have no idea of the disposition of the case. I imagine that homosexual relationships existed, but I had no firsthand knowledge of them.

On February 6 company commanders and special platoon leaders went to an area northwest of Pozzi to prepare for a planned attack north of Viareggio. It was called "Fourth Term," and it was in response to our intelligence reports that indicated the Germans intended to withdraw from Italy and have Italian Fascists rather than German troops oppose us. General Almond wanted the division to keep the German forces in Italy so that they could not assist in fighting the Russians in the East or the American and British forces in the West.

The next day, at 1830 hours, there was a meeting of the battalion commander and all of the company commanders at our battalion headquarters. I saw boyish Captain Jessie Jarman, commanding officer of I Company, and gruff Captain Brown of Company L. Captain Reedy of K Company had been transferred to regimental headquarters and been succeeded by his White executive officer, Lieutenant Brackett. While we were bivouacked in tents near Viareggio, the company commanders were given their orders and the plan of attack by Colonel Daugette. In October we had attacked Mount Cauala from Seravezza on its east side. The results were disastrous for the 3rd Battalion. This time we would attack Cauala by capturing its western foothills, designated "X," "Y," and "Z."

We soon moved from the tented area to a forward command post just behind the line of departure for the attack. On the night before the attack, I was sent to regimental headquarters to bring back about twenty replacements for our line companies. I collected them, and we started walking back to battalion headquarters late at night. As we were proceeding to the point where they would be picked up by runners from each company, artillery and machine-gun fire began passing overhead. The machine guns fired tracer bullets that left a streak of light across the sky. Tanks were also firing tracers. Some of the newly arrived replacements asked me how long I had been in combat. I told them I had been there from the very first night we went on line almost six months before. They looked at me in wonder as shells exploded in the near distance. One of the replacements talked a lot as we walked, and he told me how eager he was to get into combat. I learned his name—and just days later I learned that he had been killed by a mine. Years later I learned that many of our replacements were disciplinary problems. That was not the case with this young soldier or the rest of the replacements I brought forward that night. This soldier was ready for the adventure of being in combat. He had no fear, and the last thing he was thinking about was being killed in action.

The 365th, 366th, 371st, and 370th infantry regiments were all joined in the coastal plain near Pozzi and Querceta for the largest attack that the 92nd Division would ever be involved in. The 3rd Battalion had as its first objective an area on Mount Strettoia designated Hill X, about 450 feet high. Hills Y and Z were another 100 to 200 feet above X. The ultimate goal was to move on and capture Massa. Some of the enlisted men coined the phrase, "Yassa, we's a-goin' to Massa." I can hear that even now.

Before dawn on February 8, the longest and loudest artillery barrage I had ever heard, from all of the division's guns—the 105-mm guns from the 597th, 598th, and 599th battalions and the 155-mm guns from the 600th—was directed at the Germans' positions on Hills X, Y, and Z on the western slope of Mount Strettoia, ten miles north of division headquarters at Viareggio. The 600th Field Artillery Battalion, one of two artillery battalions whose officers were Negroes, was commanded by Lieutenant Colonel Marcus H. Ray, the highest-ranking Negro officer in the division. The bombardment seemed to go on forever before our first companies crossed their line of departure at 0600, but it lasted only about an hour, bolstered by tanks and planes. By all rights, under such a barrage the enemy should have been crippled and disorganized. The three targeted hills were home to numerous German observation points and fortified by minefields, barbed wire, steel and concrete bunkers protecting hidden artillery, and machine-gun and mortar installations prepared for interlocking fire.

Company L, under Captain Brown, led the attack through minefields from the left, and at 0645 he called in the code word "Odessa," meaning "still advancing." At 0647 he called, "We are at the base of Hill X and moving on." Company L was fired upon by machine-gun fire and small arms at 0715 but kept advancing up the hill. At 0745 Brown once again said, "Odessa." At 0805 Company L reported that they were engaging the enemy while encountering heavy machine-gun and small arms fire, but were forty to fifty yards from the top of Hill X. They had just knocked out a machine gun. At 0820 Company L was only thirty yards from the top of Hill X and had four casualties, none serious. They had captured four enemy machine guns and were sending four prisoners back to headquarters. At 0900 Company L stated, "Almost America," meaning they were almost at their objective. At 0953 Company L reported that Captain Brown was hurt. They also said that they needed more ammunition and had dug in. I Company captured Hill Y at 1400 hours. Company K captured Hill Z and dug in. Moments later Company I reported that they were crossing an open area and needed more smoke to obscure their position. At 1030 Lieutenant Brackett of Company K had lost contact with his men.

I viewed much of the attack from the battalion's forward observation post, perhaps a quarter of a mile behind the line of departure. German soldiers who survived our initial artillery bombardment staggered out of their holes and were soon captured. Battalion Headquarters Company's A&P platoon was busily blowing barbed wire with their Bangalore torpedoes and clearing mines. Suddenly, as I looked up from the forward outpost, which was a loft in a farmhouse, I saw puffs of smoke and dust begin to appear among our troops. The Germans had caught us in a trap and were shelling our attacking troops with mortars of deadly accuracy. Our assault had failed, and some of our men began to unass the hills. Napoleous Bostic of the A&P platoon was the largest man in the 3rd Battalion—over six feet six inches tall. We called him either "Big" or "Big Bostic." I saw him staggering back along the road, crying, clearly in a state of shock. He leaned on me, and I took him to the battalion aid station. I never saw "Big Bostic" again.

At 1100 hours we learned that Captain Brown was "shook up" but still in action; Lieutenant Horner and Lieutenant Johnson of L Company were wounded and had to be evacuated;

Lieutenant Thibodeaux of L Company was wounded. At 1115 Company I was on Hill X and preparing to move to Hill Y. Just after 1400 hours, I Company had captured Hill Y. At 1459 hours, Companies I and L called for litter bearers. Captain Jarman reported at 1649 hours that the situation was well in hand, but later that evening the Germans counterattacked with a heavy mortar barrage and Captain Jarman was killed. His first sergeant went out and recovered his body. At 1755 hours his successor, 1st Lieutenant John Madison, executive officer of Company I, a quiet, reserved Negro, reported that only eight men were left on Hill Y. All officers except Madison had been killed or wounded. Company K was pinned down by small arms and automatic weapons fire on the first knob of Hill Z.

At 1715 hours the enemy began shelling Hill X, and men were seen leaving their positions. Bombardments were heavy and constant from German coastal batteries at Punta Bianca. The gain for the day, reported to battalion headquarters at 1900 hours, was all of 1,000 meters. Enemy artillery was hitting our former command post at Querceta, and an engineering officer had been killed in the artillery fire. Colonel Sherman was in the battalion command post at 2115 hours. It was reported that Company I was disorganized; Company K had fifteen to twenty killed or missing; Company L had two platoons left.

In Company I, Captain Jarman's death was reported along with forty-nine wounded and four missing. K Company had three men killed, nineteen wounded, and four missing in action. M Company had twelve wounded in action. Most of L Company was reported missing in action. I went looking for them with Captain Shires, and we found many men of Company L huddled in a schoolhouse, several of them in shock. L Company's commanding officer, Captain Brown, returned to the command post and began cursing everyone in sight, including Colonel Daugette. He was obviously shell-shocked, and orders sent him back to the field hospital. He never returned to combat with our battalion. Brave and outspoken Captain Brown, the last Negro rifle company commander in the 3rd Battalion, was gone. Years later I was told he had been killed in action during the Korean War.

Eventually L Company reported three men killed, thirty-one wounded, and two missing in action.

Lieutenant Brooks was the 3rd Battalion's Negro Ammunition and Pioneer platoon leader. A tall and outgoing Texan, Brooks was our leading booby trap and mine expert. He played a significant part in getting men safely through the minefields. His expertise would cost him his life near the end of the Italian campaign in the spring of 1945.

Lieutenant Colonel Arthur H. Walker, commanding officer of the 2nd Battalion of the 371st Infantry, was killed by mortar fire on Hill X. He was a White officer.

For a time the remaining force of the 3rd Battalion consisted of only two officers and eighty enlisted men; they were ordered to reinforce troops on Hill Y north of Hill X and protect the left flank of the 371st Infantry's 3rd Battalion.

All of the officers killed or wounded in this attack were Negro company commanders or platoon leaders. It seems that they planned to be very aggressive in the attack. The cost was staggering to them and to those of us who survived.

Well after the February 8 attack, First Sergeant Graves of Company L reported that the platoon leaders were still checking their men. Graves, like me, was an ASTP man. He had been promoted quickly. I knew him well and associated with him quite a bit, both while we were in Italy and when we returned to the States. After the war he moved from his home in Alabama to Los Angeles and became a very important real estate developer in the African American community.

During the latter part of the battle that continued for three days, from February 8–10, our attack was to have been supported by air forces. However, one of our P-47s strafed our positions on or near Hills X, Y, and Z for over an hour. The fighter made several runs, obviously believing he was hitting a German position. I was on line with K Company, trying to assess their condition and report back to battalion headquarters during the strafing. The plane was so low that we could almost see the face of the pilot. Different colored flares were exploding on the ground, and I suspect he was confused. It was yet another instance of "friendly fire." Some of our men on the hills actually took off their shirts to show that they were Negro troops. However, at the speed he was flying, I doubt that he was able to recognize the color of their skin. That ugly error added to the anger and dismay of the 3rd Battalion.

On February 12, the battered survivors moved south of Pietrasanta into a reserve area at Fiumento. The attack on Hills X, Y, and Z north of Viareggio had cost the 3rd Battalion two veteran company commanders—boyish Jarman and crusty Brown—and several platoon leaders. The men were shaken and anxious to learn what kind of leadership would replace the men they had respected and followed into battle.

General George C. Marshall inspected our regiment on February 14, and on that same date fourteen men of Company I were sent to the stockade for failing to follow the order to patrol Hill X. The U.S. Army chief of staff's visit was a surprise; I believe it was the harbinger of a plan to reorganize the entire 92nd Division, an action that took place one month later.

We saw Germans up close when we captured them. None of us knew any German. I could say *"Alles ist kaput"* (which means "everything is finished") but nothing else. All they could say was, "New York; New York." The average German soldier knew that a lot of Negroes lived in New York's Harlem, and when they saw us that is probably why they were saying, "New York; New York." To which I would reply, "No, no, no ... Hollywood, Hollywood." Neither side communicated much. The prisoners were pretty pathetic. They weren't emaciated; if anything, they looked heavy—and they were docile.

In the middle of February, the battalion settled into its reserve position—training, investigating what happened during the recent battles, and working on secondary defensive positions. I was locked into the small world of the 3rd Battalion. While we were attacking Hills X, Y, and Z, we learned that the 366th Infantry had attacked along the beach front near the Cinquale Canal, which flows into the Ligurian Sea ten miles north of Viareggio. They were accompanied by tanks, but the results were a disaster. The tanks were either knocked out or mired in the sand, and the infantry was cut up. I believe that was the 366th's last combat role. There is a marble monument at the point where the Cinquale Canal runs into the sea that says, *"Linea Gotica, Settembre 1944–Abril 1945,"* commemorating our seven months of struggle against the western end of the Gothic Line.

From time to time—through all of this rest in one area and battle in another not very far away—men were sent back to the Keystone Theater in Lucca to see an American movie. The weather on the coast continued to be clear and cold.

Hills X, Y, and Z occupied us from September 1944 until the following April. We were *always* assaulting Hills X, Y, and Z. We'd capture them, lose them, regain and then lose them again. It was almost like they were in No Man's Land. All the time we knew that General Albert Kesselring was masterminding the German defense.

The morning of February 24, 1945, was clear and pleasant. At 0700 hours the companies were called and asked for a list of "men dependable in combat." Third Battalion headquarters was at Fiumetto, on the coast near Pietrasanta. I, the lowest-ranked person in the group, sat down with Captain Hugh Shires, Sergeant T. T. Davis, and First Sergeant Edward Ross to evaluate the men who it was thought would do best under fire. We considered only the men in headquarters platoon who had been in actual combat; that included the intelligence squad, some drivers, some cooks, and administrative personnel. It was a plus if they had been awarded a Combat Infantryman's Badge. I did not know why we were doing this, but I suspected a big organizational change and I was at the point where it happened. We enlisted men were never told why the reorganization was taking place. Later I talked to men from the other regiments, the 365th and the 371st, and they thought all the good men had been transferred out. We determined collectively that there were only one or two we could not recommend. Intelligence Sergeant Harris was replaced by Sergeant Robert Williams of the 365th Infantry. Williams was an outspoken, alert soldier from New York. He had been a professional photographer and commercial artist.

The battle performance of the 92nd Division continued to draw adverse comment. Lieutenant General Lucian K. Truscott released a severe evaluation of the February 8–11 attack in an official report written on March 5, 1945. Hargrove quotes the general (p. 128) as saying there was a "lack of leadership and control by company grade officers" and "infantry units were unable to advance against opposition or to hold ground against determined enemy attack, evidenced by excessive straggling— withdrawals under artillery and mortar concentration."

General Truscott concluded that "in spite of excellent and long training, excellent physical condition, superior support by artillery and air, the infantry of this (92nd) division lacks the emotional and mental stability necessary for combat. I do not believe that further training under present conditions will ever make this division into a unit capable of offensive action."

General Truscott did acknowledge that "conditions on the mountain tops were appalling. All supply was by man and mules. Casualties had to be carried out on litters, which required hours in many cases. Hot food was out of the question. Incessant cold rain not only added to discomfort, it reduced visibility almost to nothing, interfered with the scheduled air support, and vastly increased the difficulties of the attacking troops. Companies were becoming seriously reduced in strength by casualties and sickness. Morale suffers under long-continued exposure to battle and the exertion of campaign."

In his 1954 autobiography, *Command Missions: A Personal Story*, General Truscott applied the phrase "melting away" to the men of the 1st Battalion, 370th Infantry, and the 2nd Battalion, 366th Infantry. Hargrove adds that General Mark Clark "expressed a similar opinion about the 92nd Division" in his 1950 book, *Calculated Risk*, and concludes that there is no doubt that General Almond and his senior staff felt the same way.

Hargrove says (p. 129) that "the vast bulk of the infantrymen and engineers and their non-commissioned officers and commissioned junior officers who fought the battles" felt differently. "Most felt they had fought well" and believed that they were the victims of "a poorly planned and ineptly directed operation that was doomed to failure from its very inception."

In Hargrove's judgment (p. 139), Generals Truscott, Clark, and Almond "were unable to bring themselves to extend the same compassion and objectivity in evaluating the black Buffalo Soldiers as they did when analyzing white soldiers." For example, the failures of white troops to dislodge the Germans in the earlier battle at Cassino (January–May 1944) and the 875 men temporarily missing in that battle zone were somehow exempt from the criticism directed at the "stragglers" of the 92nd Division.

Finally, Hargrove adds (p. 140), "The 92nd Division was the only Division in the U.S. Forces about which published reports in magazines, newspapers, and books, such as those by Generals Clark and Truscott, referred to 'straggling' as a major problem and strongly condemned it as proof of the lack of courage and capability for combat readiness of black soldiers."

In the "Summary and Conclusions" chapter of his *The 92nd Infantry Division and the Italian Campaign During World War II* (McFarland & Company, Inc., ISBN-13:978-0-7864-1009-5), Daniel K. Gibran (p. 162) traces "the apparent failure of elements of the all-black 92nd Division to consistently engage the enemy and fight with grit and determination" to four conditions: segregation combined with apathy and distrust, lack of motivation and low morale, low levels of education, and leadership. Gibran identifies General Almond as strongly racist, egocentric, of dubious leadership ability, a poor strategist and tactician, and insensitive to and totally unaware of morale issues among his men. Segregation, Gibran says, led to mutual distrust among White officers and Black enlisted men. And certainly not to be ignored was the fact that the Negroes who formed the overwhelming majority of the 92nd Division's combat soldiers were men clearly "at the lower levels of educational attainment."

Gibran concludes (p. 165): "Given its relatively simple (sic) tasks during the war, the 92nd Infantry Division performance in combat was characterized in the main by failure yet punctuated by individual acts of heroism."

Where the truth lies about our division's performance—its successes and failures—I suspect will be a subject of conjecture or perhaps unknown forever. I must say that as just another GI, one working in the battalion headquarters nerve center, I was unaware that the army high command perceived that the men putting themselves in harm's way were failing to do the job. There appears to be little doubt, however, about General

Almond's racism and lack of history in leadership. In "Recipe for Failure: Major General Edward M. Almond and Preparation of the U.S. 92nd Infantry Division for Combat in World War II" *(The Journal of Military History.* 56, July 1992), Dale E. Wilson reports that by March 1942 Almond "had spent only three of his twenty-four years of service in troop-leading positions" and after the war General Almond said the 92nd Division's unsatisfactory performance was directly attributable to "the undependability of the average Negro soldier to operate to his maximum capability, compared to his lassitude toward his performing a task assigned. While there are exceptions to this rule, the general tendency of the Negro soldier is to avoid as much as possible." Wilson cites Almond as saying that Negroes should never again be used as combat troops: "To expect him to exhibit characteristics that are abnormal to his race is too much and not recommended by me." In *The Day of Battle: The War in Sicily and Italy*, 1943–1944 (Henry Holt and Company, New York, 2007, ISBN-13:978-0-8050-6289-2), Rick Atkinson cites a statement from an interview given by Almond as late as November 1953, in which the general said to interviewer Lee Nichols, "The white man is willing to die for patriotic reasons. The Negro is not. No white man wants to be accused of leaving the battle line. The Negro doesn't care…. People think that being from the South we don't like Negroes. Not at all. But we understand his capabilities. And we don't want to sit at the table with them"(National Archives and Records Administration, College Park, MD, Record group 329, Office of the Chief of Military History).

Perhaps it was in the character of Edward M. Almond, our division's leader—in his bone-deep and career-long opposition to integration of the military, deficiencies in leadership, and field strategies—that any shortcomings of the 92nd Division lay.

I was unaware at the time that the failure to capture Massa in early February had led General George C. Marshall—after discussions with Generals Clark and Truscott, Almond, and

Willis Crittenberger—to combine "the most reliable" of the 92nd Infantry's three regiments into one regiment and attach to it the 473rd (White) Infantry and 442nd (Japanese American) Infantry regiments. According to Goodman, "70 officers and 1,359 enlisted men holding decorations and/or Combat Infantryman Badges were transferred into the 370th Infantry from the 365th and 371st Infantry, and 52 officers and 1,264 enlisted men were transferred out."

On February 27 all of the new company commanders arrived at battalion headquarters at 2000 hours. They were as follows: Company I, Captain Moore; Company K, Captain Little; Company L, Captain Rafael. Replacing Captain Miles in Company M was Captain Mattishinski. All of the new company commanders were White. I did not know where they had come from or what experience they had. I'm sure Colonel Daugette and the other staff officers knew much more about them than I did. Other officers arrived as well—second lieutenants. Not all were White; I remember that Lieutenant Donald Clapp and Lieutenant Ford came into the companies in our battalion. Both were White, fresh-faced, and looked as if they had just come from Officer Candidate School. Lieutenant Ford wore glasses; Lieutenant Clapp was rather short and a little dumpy.

On February 28, General Marshall visited the 92nd Division to give his approval to the reorganization. It seems amazing to me that this one Negro division, out of all the army's forces, would receive this kind of attention from the general who reported directly to President Roosevelt. Looking back, it now seems that we were a very sensitive case for the army. General Almond's statements and sentiments to the effect that the White man is ready to die for patriotism and the Negro is not and that he, Almond, did not want to sit at the table with Negroes, were known to the officer cadre. They were much more concerned about all of that than those of us facing daily combat. We barely knew what was going on.

MARCH

In keeping with the reorganization plan, nearly one-half of the 3rd Battalion, 365 men, were transferred on March 1 to the 365th Infantry or the 371st Infantry. That afternoon, Truman Gibson and General Nelson, Deputy Commander of the Mediterranean Theater of Operations, visited our area. I did not see either of those distinguished guests. My father, who knew Gibson and his family, had apparently seen Gibson either in Los Angeles or Chicago on insurance company business, and Gibson had told him that he would be going to Italy to inspect the troops of the 92nd Division. My father told him to look me up, but I did not know that at the time, and we never met during Gibson's visit. I doubt that he would go looking for a mere corporal.

Reorganization continued: At 0830 hours on March 2, more of the old officers left the battalion, and at 0845 on that same day additional new officers arrived. A little later in the day, enlisted replacements from the 365th Infantry and the 371st Infantry arrived at 3rd Battalion headquarters. When the reorganization was completed, the 370th numbered 139 officers, 2,800 enlisted men, and 3 warrant officers. All Negro company commanders had been replaced by White officers.

Truman Gibson responded to continuing allegations of a high rate of straggling among Negro troops and the general failure of the 92nd Division in general to meet combat performance expectations. He suggested that replacements, most of them men with low AGCT scores, might be better trained; that racial pride be emphasized in training; that promotions be based entirely on merit. He noted that ninety percent of the division's men had scored low—Class IV or Class V—in the AGCT and had not been prepared under conditions that nurtured the development of a combative spirit. And he made clear that not all straggling had taken place among the members of the 92nd Division. His comments were damned by some prominent representatives of the Negro press as a smear and the utterings of an Uncle Tom. It was the army's Jim Crow policies, others said, that were at the heart of the problem.

During the reorganization our battalion was housed in large tents south of Viareggio. There was much discussion about inspections and training. It was during this period, while we were in reserve, that I had my second and last fight in the army. A large, muscular sergeant in the Ammunition and Pioneer platoon made it clear he did not like me. I think he felt that I was too close to the people who ran the battalion. After enduring his provocation for a while, I called him some names that I had picked up in Zoology 1A at Berkeley. Looking back, I believe I was as much at fault as he was because I was obviously intent on trying to demonstrate how educated I was. Someone suggested that we fight, and someone else found boxing gloves. I overheard Captain Shires say, "The sergeant will kill Corporal Houston." I had told Sergeant T. T. Davis that I had boxed in college, and he told the captain that I would be okay. The fight began, and I saw right away that the sergeant was very strong but didn't know a thing about boxing. A large crowd from our company had gathered around, and I heard someone say, "The headquarters guy knows how to box." I did know what I was doing, and I won. Afterward I went to the sergeant's tent and extended my hand in friendship. I believe everything was all right between us after that. I was grateful to have chosen a boxing elective as a physical education option at Berkeley. To this day I wonder where those boxing gloves came from in a combat zone.

On March 9 the battalion moved back into line and Headquarters was situated at C. Bichi (pronounced BEE-KEE). Two days later the battalion sent a combat patrol to Strettoia. My duties as we went back on line were to handle the journal entries and share responsibility for the telephone with Sergeant T. T. Davis, Corporal Benjamin V. Stewart, newly arrived Staff Sergeant Robert Williams, the intelligence sergeant, and Pfc. Robert Turner, also of the intelligence section. We would receive messages from our line companies or from regimental headquarters and record them in the journal.

Reorganization of the 370th Infantry Regiment, and especially the 3rd Battalion, did not affect me directly because I continued to do the same thing with most of the same people that I had worked with before the reorganization. I did, however, gain a really good friend in Sergeant Bob Williams.

I had been aware that our battalion had men who had been goofing off in combat. We transferred out those men who we thought were undependable and acquired men who were thought could be counted on to fight. I was sure that the new men would make us more effective.

In early and mid-March the Battalion continued to send out patrols to contact the units on our right and left in order to see what the Germans were doing. Most of the patrols were sent to Strettoia or to Hills X, Y, and Z. The Germans continued their shelling and harassing fire. On March 19, Company I reported that one man was killed by a mine.

On March 20 at 1735 hours, Division called to say that it had news of a general withdrawal by the Germans. The withdrawal, however, did not come about in our area. The Germans continued to shell us, and a patrol under Lieutenant Clapp of L Company reported that one GI had been killed in action, another was a litter case, and there were two walking wounded.

Battalion headquarters was heavily shelled on March 21. We were located in an olive grove, and one of the shells hit an olive tree, scattering shrapnel and killing our radio sergeant, Lester Lightfoot. Lightfoot had been with us since the beginning; he knew all there was to know about radios, and his loss was deeply felt. His father, on learning of his death, wrote Captain Shires, asking for details so that he could understand what happened. I don't know whether or not Shires ever answered. Lightfoot is buried in the U.S. Military Cemetery at Florence.

All mail leaving Headquarters Company was supposed to be read and censored by the company commander, Captain Shires. He would read it and then apply his signature. Over a number of weeks, I noticed that he really just put his signature on the envelope and sent it on. I began to help him by signing his name on the envelope and mailing the letter. It was several months later that he first noticed what I was doing. He said my version of his signature looked pretty good but that he would do all the signing from that time forward. Captain Shires was a good man, and we always got along.

On March 24, Colonel Daugette left for Rome on leave, and Major Verhuel, the new executive officer, was in charge. Patrolling continued, and we continued to receive reports that Germans remained on Hill X; in fact, a sniper was firing on our troops from his position there.

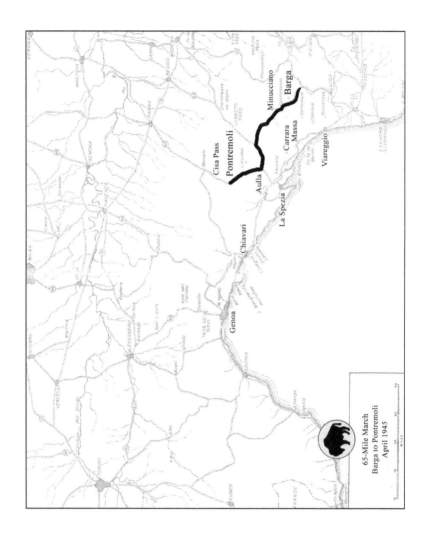

65-Mile March
Barga to Pontremoli
April 1945

APRIL

General Mark Clark, now head of the Fifteenth Army Group, arrived in our area on April 3. He spoke to the troops for ten minutes and left. We were now getting ready for a new action—hopefully, the final attack against the Germans. It was called "Second Wind," and the intent, once again, was to capture Massa. The 92nd Division would be engaged in a diversionary attack while the British Eighth and the U.S. Fifth Armies were engaged in an effort to capture Bologna, encircle German forces south of the Po River, and cross the Po to capture Verona. The major breakthrough was to be to the east of our front as our forces tried to break over the Apennine mountains into the Po Valley, while those of us in the 92nd Division, now the 442nd Infantry Regiment (Japanese American) and the 473rd Infantry (White) attacked along the coast toward Genoa.

Our diversion began on April 5. The attack on hill masses X, Y, and Z, towards Strettoia, almost immediately drew heavy mortar fire. Our infantry battalion was accompanied by three tanks. One of the tanks was disabled by a mine very early in the attack, and the other two were unable to get around it; consequently, they were stalled. On the 370th Infantry Regiment's right flank was the Japanese 442nd Infantry, and they reported that they had taken Mt. Folgorito. At 0820 hours, twelve casualties passed through the battalion aid station. The 3rd Battalion was still fighting to capture Strettoia, but was not quite there. Company K was, in fact, still not much beyond its line of departure, and Company I had been stopped by heavy mortar fire; both companies had become disorganized. Company K reported that it had nineteen casualties. Captain Moore, Company I's new commander, said that his column was split and being subjected to heavy firing.

Early in the afternoon of April 5, Company I had only a few men on Hill Z, its objective. The rest were at the foot of the hill. Also early in that afternoon, Private George York of our battalion was arrested by Private First Class Jackson, who alleged that York had left the front line. That was the only case I ever heard of in which a private arrested another private for leaving a frontline position. The information was duly recorded in our journal.

At 1400 hours, our battalion medical aides were trying to reach twenty men of L Company who had been wounded. At 1618 hours, Company I's First Platoon had a strength of twenty men; two or three had been killed in action, including Lieutenant John Madison, the only original Negro officer of that company and its executive officer. He received a posthumous Silver Star. At 1826 hours, Colonel Daugette was slightly wounded in the leg by shrapnel. At 1940 hours, the commanding general ordered that we give him the exact number of men still active in combat. The report was as follows: Company 1, 20; Company K, 45; Company L, 30; Company M, 80.

On April 6, Lieutenant Madison's death was confirmed, and it was reported that Lieutenant Clapp, the newly arrived young White officer in L Company, had also been killed. He had apparently gone into a cave to force out some Germans and was killed by machine-gun fire. The death of Lieutenant John Madison was another blow to ill-fated Company I. Killed in action from that one company were Lieutenants Ladmirault, Jones, and Madison, and Captain Jarman. Also killed in action from that company were my friends Reid, Scott, and Gray.

We had taken 25 prisoners. At 0925, we reported our strength as follows: I Company, 104; K Company, 132; L Company, 97. Company strength had been increased from the last report because men who had scattered had been found. At 1450 hours, we learned that the 442nd Infantry Regiment had taken Mt. Belvedere, overlooking Massa. Apparently, while we were engaging the enemy on the plains, the 442nd was sweeping through the mountain positions on our right flank. They had taken 106 prisoners.

On April 7, we established battalion headquarters at Querceta; the 3rd Battalion was put in regimental reserve. We heard that Lieutenant Vernon Baker, Company C, 370th Infantry, in leading his weapons platoon on April 5 and 6, had encountered the enemy near Massa and, in a series of heroic actions, had killed nine German soldiers, destroyed three enemy machine-gun positions, an observation post, and a dugout, then covered the evacuation of several of his wounded comrades. Later we learned that Lieutenant Baker had actually fought his way into Massa and radioed headquarters that he was there. He was not believed and had to fight his way back to our lines. For his action that day, Baker received the Distinguished Service Cross. Fifty-two years later, he was awarded the Medal of Honor by President Bill Clinton.

Early on the morning of April 9, I moved with other battalion headquarters personnel by truck across the Cinquale Canal. We crossed on a Bailey bridge built by our engineers and moved into a very large villa. As we approached the villa we saw fresh vehicle tracks, and inside we found food still on the table. Apparently the Germans had left only minutes before.

As I was standing in the doorway, facing inward, a loud explosion blew me ten feet inside. Explosions continued all around. I was on the floor and felt my entire back stinging. I slowly examined myself. All my arms and legs were still in place, but I discovered that a small piece of shrapnel had entered my right shoulder. The battalion medical staff was close by, so I took myself to the medical officer, Captain Young. He took off my combat jacket, shirt, and undershirt, gave me a shot of tetanus, and poured sulfa powder over the wound after removing the shrapnel. Then he wrapped me up and told me to get dressed. I looked around the large medical aid station and saw wounded men lying all over the floor. They had been brought to the aid station and just left there. The more seriously wounded were later evacuated while others like me were sent back to their units. That day I looked out from the aid station and was amazed to see the Ligurian Sea. We had fought very close to the sea for many months, but I did not know it was right there. Viareggio is on the Ligurian Sea, and I went through the city several times without noticing the water. As a result of the shrapnel wound, I was awarded the Purple Heart.

On the same day, April 9, we received an unconfirmed report that some of our troops-the 473rd Anti-Aircraft Artillery Regiment which had been converted to infantry-had passed through the 370th Infantry and had reached Massa, our battalion's longtime goal. We also learned that we were being transferred back to the Serchio Valley near Barga. The report in the journal on April 10 showed that Massa was taken at 0100 hours that morning. I felt somewhat cheated that our unit had not captured Massa. On April 11, the 442nd Infantry Regiment, having conquered severe mountainous terrain, reached and occupied Carrara. German guns at Punta Bianca, which had somehow survived our aerial and naval bombardments, continued to pound Carrara and Massa. The full force of the 679th Tank Destroyer Battalion, consisting of thirty-six 76-mm guns, was directed at Punta Bianca, and whenever the enemy fired, the battalion responded with 60 to 180 rounds. Though the barrage proved largely effective, the enemy was still firing at our troops from Punta Bianca days later.

On April 14, battalion headquarters was in Barga. We learned that day of the death of President Franklin Delano Roosevelt. For those of us still in combat and fighting for our lives, the news had no real impact. At 0845 hours that morning, nine U.S. airmen and five partisans crossed our lines from the German lines, and we ordered jeeps to send them to the rear. At 1638 hours, our intelligence officer called the A&P platoon and Company L about partisan activity that was to take place in about an hour. Three men dressed as alpine soldiers and three in civilian clothes were to pass through our lines.

On the morning of April 15, four prisoners were brought into the battalion command post, and that afternoon six German deserters were brought in and sent to the rear. Hours later, Company I reported that it had three Fascist prisoners. We were continuing to send out patrols while experiencing artillery fire.

On April 16 at 0840 hours, Company K reported seeing a large number of prisoners of war coming down the mule trail. Moments later, Company L noted that about 150 Poles, Italian civilians, Russians, and Germans were being brought in. They, too, were sent to the rear for interrogation.

On April 18, a Company K patrol reported that it had five casualties—one litter case and four walking wounded. At 1725 hours, the L Company commander reported that his patrol had found the mortar section of Company K, which had been missing for a day, idling over a *Pittsburgh Courier* newspaper. The popular and influential Negro newspaper had somehow found its way to Italy.

On April 19 our headquarters was still in Barga, and we were coordinating our movements with the 3rd Battalion of the 473rd Infantry Regiment. Our patrols were experiencing casualties, mainly from minefields, which were holding up our forward progress. At 1955, two Polish deserters reported that the Germans were pulling out their artillery.

On April 21, I was given a leave to go to Rome for four days. Company Commander Shires and First Sergeant Ross knew that I had been wounded. Even though it was not serious, they thought I deserved the leave. I joined nine or ten other soldiers from our battalion and left from battalion headquarters in Barga. An army truck took us to the railroad station in Florence, a distance of over fifty miles. We boarded an electric train for Rome and traveled through the Italian countryside, which had been devastated by the war. Many villages that we passed were in ruins, bombed out by our armies and the Germans. After a few hours, we arrived at the railroad station in Rome. We were picked up by army trucks and taken to a huge modern complex built by Benito Mussolini, *Il Duce*, and originally named for him but now called the Forum Italia. The facility was designated for use by U.S. Army enlisted personnel. It included a large indoor swimming pool and other recreational facilities, a cafeteria, and sleeping quarters that were assigned to us without regard to race. Transportation to most sites and facilities in Rome was free and provided by army trucks. The streets of Rome were empty, except for U.S. Army vehicles, a few streetcars, horse-drawn wagons, and an even fewer number of Italian Fiats, the smallest cars I had ever seen. The money we used was the lira, issued by the military. I acquired about four cartons of U.S. cigarettes and carried them with me for barter or exchange. I seldom smoked. Those of us who were interested could take free sightseeing tours to Rome's great historic sites. Tours were conducted by excellent Italian guides, paid for by the U.S. government. For us it was free. We visited the catacombs, the baths of Caracalla, the Roman Forum, the Coliseum, the Vatican, and St. Peter's Square and Basilica. We even saw the balcony where Mussolini issued his edicts and challenged the world. At night we went to nightclubs or walked up and down the Via Veneto, which was home to the U.S. Embassy and populated by scores of prostitutes and pimps. Rome was wild at night and very quiet during the day. Perhaps everyone was exhausted.

I was in Rome on Wednesday, April 25, and had been hanging out with some other Negro soldiers from the 92nd Division, when Joe Dow, another GI from Los Angeles, said, "Let's go over to St. Peter's. The Pope (Pius XII) is having his audience today." With nothing else to do, three of us went. When we got there, we picked up an Italian guide. St. Peter's, built on the ruins of a previous church, was the biggest structure I had ever seen in my life and certainly the most majestic. Our guide took us to the papal apartments, where we joined fewer than one hundred other soldiers from the various Allied armies fighting in Italy—Poles, French, Brazilians, South Africans, British, and others. The room we were taken to was hung with heavy tapestries. The Pope was carried in on a litter by his Swiss Guards and spoke with us. The thing that amazed me was that he spoke in English, he spoke in Polish because there were a lot of Polish soldiers there, and of course he spoke in Italian. In the audience there were fewer than a hundred. Even though I was not a Roman Catholic at the time, the audience with the Pope made a lasting impression on me. He was truly grateful for our presence. He gave us his blessing and sent us on our way. Our guide then took us on a tour of St. Peter's, and we even visited the Sistine Chapel, looking up to see Michelangelo's wonderful work. Under St. Peter's, an excavation was searching for the bones of the saint.

We continued to the Coliseum and walked around that famous arena, both inside and outside. At the ruins of the Roman Forum, we saw the spot where Caesar's funeral pyre was erected. Near a bridge over the Tiber River, a street artist asked if he could draw my picture for a few lire or a few cigarettes. He said he was sorry to learn that our president had died. I let him draw me and sent the picture home. I still have it and continue to find it pretty good! It is included in these pages.

It was a great leave, but soon it was over and I returned to 3rd Battalion headquarters. The route to Florence through the Italian countryside was uneventful. After we were picked up in Florence by army truck, we had a problem finding the 3rd Battalion. The front had moved north. The soldiers of the 3rd Battalion had made a sensational attack and march of more than sixty-five miles up the Serchio Valley and then northwest, capturing Pontremoli and trapping thousands of German troops along the Ligurian coast north of La Spezia. My task was to find them as our army truck drove north from Barga.

We encountered many dead German mules and destroyed vehicles along the road as we approached Pontremoli. I eventually found battalion headquarters in a prominent building overlooking the main square of the city.

The activities of the battalion during the week I was on leave in Rome were reported in a narrative prepared at battalion headquarters in hopes of earning for the battalion a unit citation. It read:

The mission of this Battalion on 21 April 1945 was to secure and organize the highly mountainous terrain north of Barga, where for months the enemy had been entrenched. The mission called for an advance of five miles on a five-mile front. By 1500 on 21 April, the Battalion had accomplished this mission but had suffered a number of casualties. Supply and evacuation was by mule and hand. This was most difficult due to the rough, mountainous terrain, width of the front, and the fact that there was no fordable point for vehicles or even mules across the Serchio River to the rear.

Late in the afternoon on 21 April, the Battalion received an order changing the mission. The Battalion was to move 18 miles during the night to Vagli di Sopra and attack at 0800 on 22 April. Assembling the Battalion, which was deployed over many miles of rough Apennine country and moving to the new attack area over steep mountainous road, was a tough, all-night job. The Battalion arrived at Vagli di Sopra at 0730, and the weary troops moved out in the attack at 0800. By 1055, the leading elements of the Battalion secured the road junction at Gramolazzo, and in spite of enemy artillery and resistance, pushed on toward their objective. By 1300 they had cleared the mountains, having advanced seven miles since 0800, and secured the Battalion objective, the highway between Minucciano and S. Michele. Minucciano is five miles north of Vagli di Sopra. Third Battalion was so far in advance of Regimental headquarters that communication was most difficult. By 1400, the Battalion made telephone contact with the Regiment and received the following mission: "Secure, as fast as possible, the important road net at Casola. To accomplish this mission will change the picture of the entire 5th Army front. Speed is essential."

The Battalion was so far in advance of other units that it was out of range of radio contact and artillery support. Supply consisted of what each man could carry. Transportation was a forgotten element, which could only be thought of after many streams had been bridged and many miles of road freed of enemy. The route of advance was over mountains, rougher, steeper, and more dangerous than any yet negotiated. As the Battalion pushed forward, it was evident that a large body of enemy was being approached. Excited civilians estimated their strength in the thousands. In spite of heavy equipment, fatigue, and rough mountains, the men pushed forward and the progress was so rapid that by 2000 hours, seven difficult mountain miles had been covered and the Battalion was poised on Mt. Cavoli overlooking Casola, the objective. The advance had taken the enemy completely by surprise. Looking down on the city and road net, scouts of the 3rd Battalion saw enemy troops and vehicles moving through up and down the roads and in the city, unmindful of the presence of the 3rd Battalion. The Battalion had both flanks exposed and was many miles in advance of all friendly troops. Just prior to dark, the Battalion commander, after a daring personal reconnaissance, gave the order to attack. Although the enemy was completely surprised, he put up a bitter and stubborn resistance with small arms, machine guns, grenades, and mortars. By 2200 the town and road net had been secured. The enemy had been driven out, captured, or killed. Enemy vehicles and a large amount of enemy equipment were taken. Although operating completely alone with no artillery support and with enemy on both flanks, front and rear, this Battalion held the road net until 1500 hours on 23 April, when another battalion moved up on the right flank.

On the night of 23 April, the 3rd Battalion was given a mission to capture Terrarossa, 20 miles away. The Battalion still had no artillery support. After the first few hours' march, which began at 2300, the column was constantly harassed by artillery that fell with deadly accuracy on the road. The march was a grueling contest. The men were worn and heavy-laden, and the road was steep. Four times during the night it was necessary to wade icy rivers, hip-deep, because all bridges had been destroyed. At daylight, fighting developed as machine gun and sniper positions were cleared. Many prisoners and much equipment was captured. At 0830, after nine hours of constant marching, the Battalion reached Aulla, where strong resistance was met. Orders had been received to bypass this resistance and capture Terrarossa as quickly as possible. A holding force was left at Aulla, while the Battalion moved over the mountain in a flanking movement on Terrarossa. After a three-mile climb, the enemy flank was attacked; and after a bitter fight, the town of Quercia was captured, enabling the Battalion to occupy high ground overlooking Terrarossa and outflanking Aulla, thus making both places useless to the enemy. On the morning of 25 April, the Battalion captured the town of Terrarossa, taking 30 prisoners and much equipment.

At 0530 on 26 April, the Battalion moved out to accomplish the most important mission to date: To capture Pontremoli and Cisa Pass, driving the enemy into the Po Valley. The Battalion had one platoon of tank destroyers attached. Artillery was still out of range. The enemy forces opposing consisted of 6,000 officers and men of the 148th German Division, seventeen pieces of artillery, several SP (self-

propelled) guns, and tanks. Besides demolishing bridges and blowing up the road, the enemy fought a delaying action until they reached the outskirts of Pontremoli, where they were organized for their last-ditch stand. They had high and favorable positions and presented a determined and stubborn resistance, which consisted of well-placed machine guns, small arms fire, artillery, and mortar, along with direct fire from SP and tanks. Only by the most skillful employment of the troops and the determined efforts of all men and officers was it made possible to drive them out. The attack was made so as to surprise the enemy and leave him to believe a much larger force confronted him. The TD Platoon was employed in a daring manner, and 81 mm mortars were used to utmost advantage by having platoon leaders help adjust fire. The Battalion commander secured the aid of 1,000 partisans and coordinated their efforts in helping clear the mountains. By the aggressive fighting spirit of all officers and men of the 3rd Battalion, the much superior enemy force was driven out of the city of Pontremoli. Three hundred prisoners and much equipment were captured. From Pontremoli, the enemy was pushed beyond Cisa Pass, the last mountain barrier south of the Po River. The entire force, after losing this important terrain feature, surrendered to the Brazilian Expeditionary Force, which had come up on the flank to cut off their retreat. This was the first large-scale surrender in Italy. The 3rd Battalion, 370th Infantry Regiment, during those seven days, had advanced 65 miles over highly mountainous terrain, captured six important objectives, and assisted in securing several others. They captured over 300 prisoners and much equipment, and delivered the final thrust that brought on this first large-scale surrender. The men and officers of the 3rd Battalion showed dauntless courage and enduring fortitude during those days, reflecting credit on the Armed Forces of the United States, and materially contributing to the success of the Allied Armies in Italy.

The 3rd Battalion's seven-day offensive march from Barga to Pontremoli may indeed have been one of the greatest marches ever made over such rugged terrain and in the face of intense enemy opposition. It outflanked the Germans on the coast and thus led to the surrender of thousands of their troops. Our long training marches in Ft. Huachuca paid off big dividends as we scaled the rugged Italian terrain. I don't believe the Germans themselves thought a battalion like ours could cover that amount of territory in such a short time. One might think that such an achievement would quell the continued criticism of Negroes in combat and surely win a unit citation, but that citation never came. One must wonder why.

I returned to duty from Rome on April 30. Although my leave in Rome was only for four days, it took three or four additional days to catch up with the frequently moved battalion headquarters. When I arrived at headquarters I learned that, on the day before, Benito Mussolini and his mistress were caught in the mountains of Northern Italy while trying to make their way to Switzerland. They were hanged in a service station in Milan.

I arrived in Pontremoli and found the battalion headquarters in a very prominent building at the city square overlooking the piazza. I learned that Bologna had fallen to our Fifth Army on April 21, and the army was moving toward the Po River. I also learned that Lieutenant Brooks, platoon leader of the Ammunition and Pioneer platoon and our booby-trap expert, had been killed in an explosion on April 25. Lieutenant Brooks was a Texan whose younger brother served with us in the 92nd Division and was an ASTP soldier. Lieutenant Brooks had commanded the respect of Colonel Daugette—and both White and Negro enlisted men alike—because he was always out in front. His men looked for mines and carried Bangalore torpedoes that blew up barbed wire, enabling the troops to get through. He was in many ways indispensable. Recently I spoke with Harry Cox, the officer in charge of the battalion's 81-mm mortars about the final moments in Lieutenant Brooks's life. Cox told me that the battalion had just captured a large depot thought to be filled with German ammunition. Brooks went over to Cox and said, "Let's go see what's there." Cox said okay. As they neared the depot, Cox said he was going to get his jeep. Brooks walked into the depot as Cox turned back. There was a tremendous explosion that knocked Cox to the ground and completely destroyed the ammunition depot. Brooks's body was never found.

MAY

At 1920 hours on May 2, the battalion received word that the war in Italy was over. The battalion journal notes, "Finito le Guerra in Italy." The night the war ended, there was much celebration in battalion headquarters and even more out in the streets of Pontremoli. Partisans and others were firing guns, and crowds were drinking wine. The whole scene was wild. The Italian citizens of Pontremoli called for our commanding officer, Colonel Daugette, to come out onto the balcony of our headquarters and greet the civilians. The colonel was somewhat reluctant to do that because the Italians were really wild at the end of the war and were shooting everywhere in their jubilation. In fact, some of them shot against walls and the bullets ricocheted and hit the person who had fired. However, Colonel Daugette did eventually step out onto the balcony, where he was cheered passionately by the Italians.

Just a few days later, on May 7, at 1630 hours I noted in the battalion journal, "The war in Europe is over!"

After we left Pontremoli, we went to Chiavari and were quartered in a very nice house. One day Sergeant Bob Williams and I were looking through the house and saw an Italian at the rear of the property. It turned out that it was his home, and he was searching for family photos. We found some that showed him in a Fascist uniform. We said, "Ah, *tu Fascisti*." And he said,

"Oh, no, no, no, no." We pointed to the pictures, laughed, and let him take the pictures and leave. Northern Italy was full of Fascists.

We stayed in Chiavari until June and then returned to the area south of Viareggio that we called Tent City. On May 14, 1945, according to Ulysses Lee (p. 588–89), Lieutenant Colonel Marcus H. Ray of the 600th Field Artillery Battalion wrote to Truman Gibson in response to Gibson's earlier report that the 92nd Division suffered from bad morale and inadequate training for combat. Ray said: "It is my considered opinion that the 92nd, at the best, was doomed to a mediocre performance of combat duties from its very inception. The undercurrent of racial antipathies, mistrusts and preconceived prejudices made for an unhealthy beginning. The failure to promote worthwhile Negroes and the giving of preferred assignments to white officers made for logical resentments. I do not believe that enough thought was given to the selection of white officers to serve with the 92nd and further, that the common American error was made of assuming that Southern white men understand Negroes. Mixed units as we have known them have been a dismal failure. In white officered units, those men who fit into the Southern pattern are pushed and promoted regardless of capabilities and those Negroes who exhibit the manliness, self-reliance, and self-respect which are the 'sine qua non' in white units, are humiliated and discouraged. In the two Artillery Battalions of the Division, officered by Negroes, it was necessary to reduce large numbers of non-commissioned officers because they held rank only because they fitted the 'pattern.' Their subordinates resented and disrespected them— justly so. I was astounded by the willingness of the white officers who preceded us to place their own lives in a hazardous position in order to have tractable Negroes around them.

"In the main I don't believe the junior officers guilty of faulty judgment or responsible for tactical failures. Soldiers do as ordered but when plans sent to them for execution from higher headquarters are incomplete, inaccurate, and unintelligible, there is inevitable confusion. The method of selection and the thoroughness of the training in the Officer Candidate Schools weeded out the unfit and the unintelligent with but rare exceptions but the polishing of the officer after graduation was the duty of his senior officers. In mixed units, this, manifestly, has been impossible. I believe that the young Negro officer represents the best we have to offer and under proper, sympathetic and capable leadership would have developed and performed equally with any other racial group. Therefore, I feel that those who performed in a superior manner and those who died in the proper performance of their assigned duties are our men of the decade and all honor should be paid them. They were Americans before all else. Racially, we have been the victims of an unfortunate chain of circumstances backgrounded by the unchanged American attitude as regards the proper 'place' of the Negro. . . .Perhaps from your vantage point, where you see the worldwide picture, it is not as dismal as my rather restricted view based mainly on the 92nd Division. I do not believe the 92nd a complete failure as a combat unit but when I think of what might have been, I am heart sick. . . ."

I believe Colonel Ray's comments are an excellent summary of what happened to the 92nd Division. However, the colonel wrote as an artillery officer, and I write as a (then) corporal in the infantry who was present when the actions that resulted in much of the criticism occurred. Ray lays much of the blame on the "unchanged American attitude" concerning the proper place of the Negro. His comment is correct, but polite. I agree with those Negro leaders at the time who said it was Jim Crow and not a lack of education or adequate training that affected our division's performance. We were fighting the Nazis and Italian Fascists with one hand and Jim Crow with the other. Many of us from the North, East, and West had never encountered the kind of racial discrimination and segregation we faced in the army. Soldiers from the South knew what segregation and discrimination were really about, and many of those rural young men with low test scores who formed our ranks felt they were often being sent on suicide missions. We were hobbled by stragglers, yes, but we fought on and in the last weeks of the war achieved a remarkable victory with our sixty-five-mile march through the Apennines from Barga to Pontremoli. We defeated the Nazis and Italian Fascists, causing thousands of them to surrender, but we did not conquer Jim Crow.

JUNE

On June 6, 1945, one year after D-Day in Normandy and one month after the end of the war in Europe, the 370th Infantry Regiment, together with other units from the 92nd Division, had the honor of escorting the ashes of Christopher Columbus back to Genoa from where they had been hidden by the partisans during the war. The men of Company H of the 370th Infantry Regiment accompanied the ornamental urn, which rested on a horse-drawn carriage, into the Piazza della Vittoria, largest square in Genoa. Commanded by Captain Harold Montgomery, the men of Company H, one of the regiment's heavy weapons companies, walked at a funeral cadence in a manner that I have seen only Negro troops perform. Montgomery was a tall man and very handsome, and he was one of the regiment's outstanding leaders. (Later, he was one of the officers who founded the World War II 92nd Infantry Division Association.) The day was hot. Commanding General Almond spoke to the troops and assembled Italian citizens, the famous Negro choir, "Wings Over Jordan," sang in the ceremony, and the division chaplain added appropriate words. Some of the men in the regiment fainted from the heat before the ceremony was over. If you stand at attention for a very long time, you must be certain to bend your knees slightly; otherwise, the blood supply is cut off and you can pass out.

I later learned that no one is really certain whether or not those were truly Columbus's ashes. His remains have been variously reported to be in Seville, Spain; in Havana, Cuba; and in the Dominican Republic. However, the ceremony certainly was stirring, and it was quite an honor to those of us who had fought for such a long time under a great cloud of alleged incompetence.

In 1995, in celebration of the fiftieth anniversary of the end of the war in Italy, the Italians invited Harold Montgomery and other members of the 92nd Infantry Division Association back to Genoa for a celebration. The men were wildly cheered when they were introduced at a soccer game.

After the June 6, 1945, ceremony, the 3rd Battalion returned to its headquarters in Chiavari. We stayed a few more days in the house that was owned by the Fascist that Bob Williams and I had seen trying to remove photos of himself in his black Fascist uniform. Then we moved back to the army tent city south of Viareggio. It was there that the Fifth Army or our own commanding officers made a huge mistake in judgment: one evening while we were going through the chow line, we were told that we were each being given cognac from the German Army's liquor supply. Each canteen cup was filled with strong cognac, and that night was absolutely crazy. We were all pretty drunk; it's a wonder that no one was killed.

After we had been in Tent City a few days, soldiers who had been in the army for a long time began to be given leave to return home to the States. First Sergeant Ross, Battalion Sergeant Major Boyette, and Operations Sergeant Davis were high on that list. They began to leave. When Boyette left, I was promoted to sergeant and then, just a few weeks later, to staff sergeant—three stripes above and one below—and told that I would be the sergeant major. The battalion sergeant major rank is usually a tech sergeant. The sergeant major is the enlisted man in the battalion who handles all of the administrative duties. All information flows through him; he, in turn, working through the battalion clerk, creates all of the reports that have come from information passed down from division, regiment, and battalion headquarters to the companies. My promotion brought me an additional $10 a month. With my rank and Combat Infantryman's Badge, my pay was about $130 per month maximum during my term of service.

THE FINAL DAYS AND HEADING HOME

Toward the end of June 1945, army headquarters gave the 3rd Battalion a new assignment. We would guard the Port of Naples. We boarded wooden freight cars near Viareggio and began a slow and very uncomfortable trip south to Naples. We ate and slept in those cars. When we got to Rome, we got out and, in army style, without shirts, ran around the outside of the ancient Coliseum. Then we resumed our trip south and passed through the ruins of Cassino. The battle for that city had occurred more than a year before, but Cassino was still rubble. We finally arrived at our destination: another army-constructed tent city near the port.

There was not much recreation in Naples. It was a very dirty city, and the people were poor. I took a day trip to Pompeii to see its ruins. I knew it had been destroyed in A.D. 79 by the eruption of Mount Vesuvius. Vesuvius hovered over the port and was still smoking from its most recent eruption. An expert guide took us through Pompeii. We saw how the Romans ate, their plumbing system, their baths, their erotic art, and, of course, their brothels. A flying cock-and-balls was imbedded in stone, pointing to the brothels. Vendors were trying to sell us lead cock-and-balls that could be hung around the neck. Amazing!

After we left Pompeii and were on our way back to Naples, we stopped at a cameo factory where we could buy gifts to take home.

In Naples, Bob Williams and I went to the San Carlo Opera House and saw a ballet. It was a real treat and quite a change from the drabness and dirt that was everywhere. The food in Naples was terrible. We ate canned tongue, fixed many different ways for breakfast, lunch, and dinner. I think a boatload of tongue must have been the entire cargo of the only ship that had yet landed at the port. I soon became ill and could keep nothing on my stomach. I had never been to a doctor for an illness, but I went this time. He gave me a large pill, and the next day I was fine. The other guys just laughed and said I was given a horse pill.

In early August, our battalion was permitted to send a few soldiers to Nice, France, for a seven-day leave. As battalion sergeant major, I decided that I would be one of the soldiers to go. We boarded an army truck and started north to Leghorn (Livorno). We stopped in Rome for the night and then continued the next day. We got to Leghorn and boarded a rusty old ship called the *Vulcan*. There were no toilets on the ship, and everything had to be done overboard in the wind. It was an overnight trip. I attempted to make friends with a French Senegalese soldier who was also on leave. He spoke French, Senegalese, and some Italian. We bonded briefly, but the language barrier kept us from learning very much about each other, and we soon went our separate ways. The Allied armies in Italy were multinational and multiethnic.

After we docked in Nice, we were picked up by army truck and taken to our hotel, the Ruhl. It was a first-class hotel, right on the Promenade des Anglais, looking out to sea. Three of us Negroes were assigned to a luxurious room. My two roommates were not from the 92nd Division. After we adjusted to the hotel, we went out to see the sights and were met by a Black French entertainer, Jimmy Coco, who said he would show us the town, but first he wanted us to see his apartment. Since there were three of us, we agreed to accompany him. When we arrived, we were greeted by a middle-aged French woman who asked us, "Well, who wants to go first?" All three of us were out of there in less than thirty seconds. Mr. Coco obviously doubled as pimp.

While in Nice, I swam in the very blue Mediterranean Sea, just across from the famous Hotel Negresco. The water felt great, but there were none of the large waves I was used to from my days at the Ink Well at Santa Monica Beach near my Los Angeles home. We used to body surf there. The beaches in Los Angeles were segregated; as a result, we designated our stretch of beach between Bay and Bicknell Streets the Ink Spot. The water there became known as the Ink Well.

A motor launch in Nice took us along the shore so that we could see the nearby principality of Monaco. One evening, at one of the hotels in Nice, we were entertained by Maurice Chevalier, the great French performer. It was his first appearance since the war ended, and he was trying to erase the suspicion and charges that he had collaborated with the Nazis. He sang all night and told us how much he loved us Americans and how much he loved France. All in all it was a great show, and he received many standing ovations.

I took side trips to the French countryside and visited an area where perfume was made. More exciting was meeting two soldiers from home. I was looking out to sea when I saw another Negro soldier doing the same thing. It was Nolan Payton. Nolan and his brother had both worked for Golden State Mutual Life Insurance Company, which my father had helped organize and run as one of its principal officers. Nolan was a sergeant and ran an army post exchange somewhere in France. We talked for a long time and then ran into another Negro soldier from Los Angeles, Hal Sinclair. Hal had been an outstanding sprinter at UCLA before the war. We three did some sightseeing together and had a thoroughly good time. Those chance meetings were a wonderful coincidence.

After seven great days, my leave ended and I took the *Vulcan* back to Leghorn and an army truck south to Naples. My new company commander was not too happy that I had been away for a little more than seven days. I think that in my absence he was forced to do some of the administrative work that was the responsibility of the sergeant major. As a result, I did not get my fifth stripe and did not become a technical sergeant.

While we were on guard duty at the Port of Naples, there was continual talk about the forthcoming invasion of Japan. Some units were being sent to the Pacific through the Panama Canal. We heard that casualties were expected to be over one million and that the bulk of casualties would be from the infantry. The atomic bombs dropped on Hiroshima and Nagasaki ended the war for us. We didn't even have to think about being in the invasion of Japan. We only had to think about going home.

The point system developed by the army to send soldiers back to the states for discharge included points for length of time in the army, number of months overseas, and wounds (Purple Hearts) received in action against the enemy. I remembered that each Purple Heart added five points, and that helped in my case since I had been in the army a relatively short period of time in comparison with others.

We left Naples near the end of September and moved to a tent camp near Pisa. While there, another soldier and I drove a short distance to the famed tower. Few people were around so we climbed the famous edifice. The passageways inside were narrow, and a reckless person might tumble off the sides, which were quite open. We reached the top, where there were bells and a flagpole, and I decided to put my mark on that flagpole alongside numerous others. Perhaps it is there yet.

Some of the members of the 92nd Division who had been in the ASTP and did not have many points enrolled in the University of Florence and took courses. One such soldier was Les Shaw. Some years after the war, Les and I became very good friends, and he later became the first Black postmaster for the city of Los Angeles. Meanwhile all of us tried to keep busy with athletics, orientations, and training. The short-arm inspections continued.

I was eventually notified that a group of us would leave for the states on November 12, 1945. We were to be quarantined for two weeks prior to sailing from Leghorn because the army did not want any diseases carried to the states. A short-arm inspection, just before we were to board, showed that even the quarantine was not one hundred percent effective. Some of the men were infected.

We boarded the *Frostburg Victory*, a hastily built troop transport, and were assigned bunks. My bunk was on top of three others, near a light that burned twenty-four hours a day. Just before we sailed, we were all topside. The ship's horn was just getting ready to blow, and the steam sounded like an incoming artillery shell. All of us hit the deck: the effects of combat had not worn off. We set sail on a very calm Mediterranean Sea, and in the next two days all of us, including the crew, became sick. It was a mess. We would eat and then rush to the sides or to the head. As soon as we passed the Rock of Gibraltar and sailed into a very rough Atlantic Ocean, we all got well. The waves in the Atlantic were huge, and the Frostburg Victory felt like a roller coaster. I did a lot of reading on that crossing. Most of us on the ship were from the 92nd Division, and for a while there was a rumor that we were going to land in New York and participate in a victory parade in Harlem. That, however, proved not to be the case.

On November 27, we landed at Hampton Roads, Virginia, and were immediately taken to Camp Patrick Henry, the same camp we had departed from seventeen months before. I telephoned my father and told him that I was back in the states and would probably be home in a week or so. I asked him to call my mother with the news. He told me that the president and founder of the insurance company he had helped organize had died and that he was the new president of Golden State Mutual Life Insurance Company.

We did not stay long in Camp Patrick Henry. The very next day we boarded a troop train, traveling coach, and headed west. I do not know what cities we went through. We seemed to be dropping off railroad cars and adding some as we went along. The train went directly through Los Angeles to Fort MacArthur, California, the army base where I had entered the service. We arrived in the morning and immediately began our discharge processing. All the papers were ready, and the men and women working to discharge us from the army seemed very efficient. At one point, when I was very near the end of the process, an officer saw that I had received the Purple Heart and asked if I wished to make a claim. He said it would not take too much time. I thought for about two seconds and told him to continue my discharge process. The shoulder where I had been hit by shrapnel was okay. I did not realize at that time that my hearing had been affected by constant explosions and by being in the muzzle blast of heavy artillery. Many years later, I did receive compensation for that disability. I received my final pay, my discharge papers, and $200 in cash.

I left the army on the evening of December 5, 1945, and took a Pacific Electric train to downtown Los Angeles and a streetcar to the stop very near my mother's house. It was nearly midnight when I rang the bell, and my grandmother and mother opened the door. I was home.

EPILOGUE

The Los Angeles I returned to after the war was a new city. It had been overrun by Negroes from the South seeking to escape racial segregation and find meaningful employment in the nation's war industries, where by presidential order racial discrimination had been banned. Many garages in the Negro community had been converted into living quarters. Little Tokyo, in the heart of downtown Los Angeles, had become the residence of many Negro defense workers while the former Japanese American citizen-residents of that community and others in Los Angeles and beyond spent their days in any of ten distant relocation camps.

All of my Los Angeles friends who had served in the military returned home safely. None of us talked about the war and what we had done except for an occasional, "I bumped into Nolan in Paris," or "I was landing planes on an aircraft carrier." A number of Negro Angelenos had served in India, and from time to time they might mention that, but only briefly. We talked mostly about getting an education (the GI Bill of Rights made that possible for many who previously had thought the expense of a college education inconceivable), about getting a job, about girls, and about getting married. Racially restrictive covenants, the law at that time, kept us living in the same general neighborhood we had left to join the military.

I resumed my relationship with Philippa Jones, whom I had met on the campus at UCLA. She was in art school and worked for her father, Phil Jones, who distributed along the West Coast all of the nationally famous Negro publications, including *Negro Digest, Ebony, Jet*, the *Chicago Defender*, and the *Pittsburgh Courier*.

Two months after my discharge, I said good-bye temporarily to Philippa and headed north alone to begin the new semester at UC Berkeley. I moved back into the Oxford Hall cooperative dormitory. Two Jewish brothers, Bernard and "Red" Linsky, had lived near me in Oxford Hall before I left for the service. Now someone told me that "Red" Linsky had been killed fighting in Palestine. John Stair, the president of my high-school class, had been killed testing a secret new airplane over the Mojave Desert. It was many years before I learned that Magellan C. ("Crip") Mars, my camp counselor at the 28th Street Y in Los Angeles, had been killed in combat as a member of the 92nd Division.

Philippa and I eloped and were married on July 15, 1946, in Santa Ana, California. She continued to live with her parents. The first of our three children, daughter Pam, was born in 1947, and I graduated from Cal in February 1948. I returned to Los Angeles and began my working career as an accountant with Golden State Mutual Life Insurance Company. Two other children, a second daughter and then a son, followed. I spent my entire career in the insurance business. Over the next several decades, I was directly involved in integrating some of America's largest corporations, in the civil rights movement, the Catholic Interracial Council, and the United Way, and had a significant hand in convincing top life insurance executives to embrace corporate social responsibility.

As the years passed, the war slowly receded into memory. My closest army friends, the six-member intelligence squad, had returned to civilian life and, with rare exception, I never heard from any of them again. Very few Californians were in the 92nd

Division, and those of us who served in Italy never saw each other after the war—with one exception: the mortar master, Harry Cox. He and I talked from time to time about our experiences in Italy. Harry passed away in 2008. Harry was an officer and a friend of Reuben Horner, our battalion's greatest hero, and Vernon Baker, the only member of our division to receive the Medal of Honor. Looking back over a distance of more than sixty years, it is clear to me that those of us in the 3rd Battalion, 370th Infantry, 92nd Infantry Division, fought the war as second-class citizens. I personally encountered no racism during my combat experience. No one ever called me the N word, nor did I hear a slur of any kind. But in the United States of America during World War II, racial discrimination and segregation were ever present. My brother Norman first experienced the army's severe racial discrimination while in the ROTC at the University of California at Berkeley. He quickly rose to the position of platoon sergeant and should have been promoted to officer status. His ROTC captain was told that he was to inform Norman that he was "too heavy." At five feet eleven inches and 180 pounds, the charge was ridiculous. That same captain later told me what had happened and said it was a shame. At Camp Van Dorn in Centreville, Mississippi, Norman became a platoon sergeant in the Quartermaster Corps and applied for Officer Candidate School. The camp commander, a Southerner, called him in and told him outright that "no Nigra [from his camp] would ever be sent to Officer Candidate School." After his service in the China-Burma-India theater of operations, Norman returned to civilian life, rose to the presidency of the Los Angeles branch of the NAACP, and marched with Dr. Martin Luther King Jr. at Selma, Alabama.

The armed forces in which I served relegated most Negroes to service units in support of the combat forces but never really wanted to place them in direct combat. We of the 92nd Infantry Division were one of the few exceptions. We fought the Nazis and the Fascists with honor, face-to-face in the rugged mountains of Italy. We suffered hundreds of casualties and in the end defeated the Nazi proponents of a master race and their allies. Yet the heart of America did not change toward its Negro soldiers or its Negro citizens. When we returned, we encountered the same segregation and discrimination that had existed since the end of the Civil War. Nothing had changed.

I asked one of my oldest friends, who had lived with me in the co-ops at Cal Berkeley and served in the army, just what did we as Negroes gain from the war. He said, in no uncertain terms, "We didn't gain crap!" I asked another friend, who had graduated from Cal Berkeley as an engineer and served as a diesel engineer in the Merchant Marines during the war, the same question. He told me that when he returned to civilian life he tried to get a job as a diesel engineer but was told they weren't hiring Negroes. For a time after the war, he worked instead as a janitor. The Tuskegee Airmen, who escorted allied bombers on their runs all over Europe from their base in Italy, could not even think of getting a job flying a commercial passenger plane in the United States. That is what we came home to. When, as a young married man, I tried to move into the married students' dormitories at Cal Berkeley in 1947, I was provided an apartment with the Negro shipyard workers in Richmond, California, several miles from the campus. (*Note:* By that time I was a three-year letterman in track and field and a member of Cal's prestigious Order of the Golden Bear.) Philippa, baby daughter Pam, and I had a pretty good time in what we called "the Projects." The people there were all from the Deep South, and I almost felt that I was back in the army. A train running right behind our housing unit rattled dishes about every hour.

In retrospect I am amazed at what we men of the 92nd Division accomplished. We were fighting to defeat Nazi Germany, and we were fighting to free the Italians, who were the real victims of the war in Italy. We won the hearts and the minds of those that we freed. You could see it in their eyes and gestures. You could feel it in their voices and hearts as we captured town after town, village after village. They loved us and showered us with hugs, kisses, and wine. Our color was no issue at all, and they were not critics.

In 1978, Philippa and I visited Italy for the first time since the end of the war. We rented a car in Paris and drove to Italy. Naturally we stayed in Viareggio, since that had been the headquarters of the 92nd Division. Walking in the little shops that dot the beachside, we came to an artist's studio. Philippa, an artist herself, said, "Let's go in." The artist was there; and as we looked around, I said to him in Italian, "I was here in 1944 and 1945." He was a big, gruff-looking Italian, and he said, "*Tu Buffalo.*" I said, "*Sì.*" He started hugging and kissing me with the great emotion common to Italians. He opened his wallet and pulled out an old card that identified him as a partisan. His name was Bruno Tintori, and he described how he had helped us carry ammunition over the mountains. He took us next door to a bar, introduced us to his friends, and we talked and drank grappa the rest of the afternoon. Bruno Tintori is now dead, but I later learned that he had become one of Italy's most famous contemporary artists.

Bruno Tintori's expression of gratitude for what the Buffalo Soldiers had done for Italy, fighting in the rugged North Apennine mountains and freeing them from the yoke of Fascism and Nazism, will always be remembered. To the Italians we were first class. To the Italians we were heroes.

APPENDICES

CHAIN OF COMMAND AND OUR DIVISION'S COMPONENTS

The chain of command of the United States Army is complex and consists of several strata. For readers unfamiliar with the organization, it may be helpful to explain the various army units, their approximate size, and their leadership:

Army: 50,000 or more soldiers, usually commanded by a lieutenant general or higher, and consisting of two or more corps.

Corps: 20,000–45,000 soldiers, made up of two to five divisions and typically led by a lieutenant general.

Division: 10,000–15,000 soldiers, formed into three regiments and commanded by a major general.

Regiment: As many as 5,000 soldiers formed into two to five battalions. Usually commanded by a colonel. Brigades are similar to regiments.

Battalion: 300–1000 soldiers divided into four to six companies, normally commanded by a lieutenant colonel.

Company: 62–190 soldiers divided into three to five platoons. Companies are normally led by a captain, with a first sergeant serving as principal assistant.

Platoon: 16–44 soldiers, led by a lieutenant and consisting of two to four squads or sections.

Squad: 9–12 soldiers, usually commanded by a sergeant or staff sergeant.

The three infantry regiments of the 92nd Division were the 365th, 371st, and 370th. I was a member of the 370th's 3rd Battalion, which included Companies I, K, L, and M, and Headquarters Company. The 92nd Division also included the 597th, 598th, 599th, and 600th Field Artillery Battalions. The 597th, 598th, and 599th were attached to infantry regiments. The 600th was called the division's artillery and, unlike the other battalions, which fired 105-mm howitzers, it fired 155-mm guns. All of the enlisted men and most of the artillery officers were Negroes, as were the medical officers and chaplains. Lieutenant Colonel Marcus Ray, whose trenchant comments on the performance of the Negro in combat appear in this text, commanded the 600th. In addition to infantry regiments and artillery battalions, the 317th Medical Battalion, the 317th Engineer Battalion, the Reconnaissance Company, and a company of military police were all part of the 92nd Division.

General Orders Number 14, Headquarters 92nd Infantry Division, dated 14 April 1944, created Combat Team 370 under the command of Colonel Raymond G. Sherman. Upon reaching the front lines in Italy, we were attached to IV Corps of the Fifth Army headed by General Mark W. Clark. Our affiliated combat units were the 598th Field Artillery Battalion, a company from the 317th Engineering Battalion, and a company from the 317th Medical Battalion.

The 3rd Battalion began its combat activities in Italy in August 1944 with 854 men.

SENIOR OFFICERS IN THIS BOOK

Major General Edward M. Almond (1892–1979), commanding general, 92nd Infantry Division

Major General Vernon Prichard, commanding general, 1st Armored Division

Colonel Raymond G. Sherman, commander, 370th Infantry Regiment

Lieutenant Colonel Clarence W. Daugette Jr., commanding officer, 3rd Battalion

Major Sturdevant, Executive Officer

Captain Hugh D. Shires, commanding officer, Headquarters Company, S-1

Captain Jesse Jarman, commanding officer, I Company, 3rd Battalion

Captain Elmer Reedy, commanding officer, K Company, 3rd Battalion

Captain Clarence Brown, commanding officer, L Company, 3rd Battalion

Captain Julian Miles, commanding officer, M Company, 3rd Battalion

Staff Sergeant Thomas T. Davis, operations sergeant, 3rd Battalion

Captain Nathan Roane, operations officer (S-3), later executive officer, Headquarters Battalion; Captain Lemuel Price succeeded Roane as S-3

First Lieutenant Harrington, intelligence officer, S-2

ABOUT THE AUTHOR

Ivan J. Houston is a graduate of the University of California at Berkeley. He entered the University in 1942, left to serve in the army from 1943 until 1945, and returned to receive his B.S. degree in 1948. From 1970 to 1990, he served as the chief executive officer of Golden State Mutual Life Insurance Company, one of the nation's largest African American businesses, and he was named one of the 100 Most Influential Black Americans by *Ebony* magazine.

Mr. Houston has served on many corporate boards, including Broadway Federal Bank, Pacific Telesis Corporation, Kaiser Aluminum and Chemical Corporation, First Interstate Bank, and Metromedia. In service to his community, he has been a member of the board of Regents of Loyola Marymount University, a trustee of the Claremont Colleges, the Catholic University of America, and a member of the business advisory board of both the UC Berkeley Business School and the Anderson School of Management at UCLA. He has served as president of the Los Angeles City Human Relations Commission, as chairman of the Los Angeles Urban League, and as trustee for the National Urban League. He has also been a board member of the American College of Life Underwriters and served as chairman of the Life Office Management Association.

Mr. Houston holds an honorary Doctor of Laws degree from LaVerne University, the Brotherhood Award from the National Council of Christians and Jews, and the Cardinal's Award from the Archdiocese of Los Angeles. Pope John Paul II named him a Knight of the Order of St. Gregory the Great.

INDEX

Website
www.blackwarriorsbook.com